THE BLUEPRINT

THE BLUEPRINT

A Plan for Living Above Life's Storms

KIRK FRANKLIN

with Nick Chiles

GOTHAM BOOKS

Published by Penguin Group (USA) Inc.
375 Hudson Street, New York, New York 10014, U.S.A.
Penguin Group (Canada), 90 Eglinton Avenue East, Suite 700, Toronto, Ontario M4P
2Y3, Canada (a division of Pearson Penguin Canada Inc.) • Penguin Books Ltd, 80 Strand,
London WC2R 0RL, England • Penguin Ireland, 25 St Stephen's Green, Dublin 2, Ireland
(a division of Penguin Books Ltd) • Penguin Group (Australia), 250 Camberwell Road,
Camberwell, Victoria 3124, Australia (a division of Pearson Australia Group Pty Ltd) •
Penguin Books India Pvt Ltd, 11 Community Centre, Panchsheel Park, New Delhi—110
017, India • Penguin Group (NZ), 67 Apollo Drive, Rosedale, North Shore 0632, New
Zealand (a division of Pearson New Zealand Ltd) • Penguin Books (South Africa) (Pty)
Ltd, 24 Sturdee Avenue, Rosebank, Johannesburg 2196, South Africa

Penguin Books Ltd, Registered Offices:
80 Strand, London WC2R 0RL, England

Published by Gotham Books, a member of Penguin Group (USA) Inc.

First printing, May 2010
1   3   5   7   9   10   8   6   4   2

Gotham Books and the skyscraper logo are trademarks of Penguin Group (USA) Inc.

LIBRARY OF CONGRESS CATALOGING-IN-PUBLICATION DATA

Franklin, Kirk, 1970–
The blueprint : a plan for living above life's storms / Kirk Franklin.
p. cm.
ISBN 978-1-59240-547-3 (hardcover)
1. Christian life. I. Title.
BV4501.3.F7355 2010
248.4—dc22   2010004921

Printed in the United States of America
Set in ITC Galliard • Designed by Elke Sigal

I dedicate this book to my father-in-law, Bill Collins,
and my father in the faith, Tony Evans. Whatever I lost
as a child, you helped me find it as a man. Thank you.

Contents

Introduction

Imagine waking up Christmas morning and receiving an expensive gift under the tree. It's nicely wrapped, beautifully presented. You tear off the paper, dig through the little Styrofoam peanuts, and find the gift. But it needs assembling. So you continue to dig. You dig and dig until frustration sets in. When you finally get to the bottom of the box, there's no instruction manual. So now you're left with lots of pieces spread out all over your floor and you have no directions for putting them together.

This takes all the joy out of the day. Your holiday is unfinished. You have a chaos of parts, with no plan for putting them together. You're on your own to turn the chaos into the pretty picture on the box. What're you going to do?

For too many of us, our lives look like the same chaos of parts that we sometimes face on Christmas morning. The parts are scattered everywhere, our future is dark and cloudy, and we have no manual to put things together. So what do we do? Where do we turn? One option is to copy the kid across the street. Or maybe we look for answers with the guy on the corner. Or the thug on TV. Or the preacher in the pulpit. Because we think their gifts came with manuals. But in truth, they had no blueprints either. They put their stuff together by copying others, who had copied still other people before them—just like you are thinking of copying the ones before you. So what should you do? Do you copy the copies of copies, perpetuating the fraud? Do you fake it? Just grab everything, dump it all together and pray something fits? Do you give up and throw the whole mess away? Or maybe you walk away, leaving the pieces spread out everywhere.

You've been given a gift. But without the instruction manual, without the proper plans, that gift loses its value. It's practically worthless. So if you're going to get anything out of it, you need a blueprint. And as things go with Christmas presents, so they also go with life. The greatest Giver of all has given you a precious gift—your life. And in order for that gift to be truly valuable to you, you need a blueprint.

But before we start the journey, I want to thank you for taking this ride with me. I know there are a lot of other books out there trying to "ooh" and "aah" you with their religious rhetoric and spiritual talk, trying to preach to you about the right way to live. I am 100 percent, unapologetically Christian. Jesus is my hero for real. My outlook and observations are sprinkled with my love for my faith. But I am also aware that, for centuries, we Christians have not always done a good job living what we preach. So for those who think this is going to be a soft, cuddly "pie in the sky" Bible book, don't get it twisted. It's one thing to tell someone they can make it, but it's another (and more important) thing to tell them as best you can *how* to make it, *how* to get over the barriers that have been there for years.

Because of my background and everything I've been through (which you'll hear more about later), I am very passionate about being honest, straight up, and transparent about my struggles as a black man, my lack of education, my frustrations with the church that I am so proudly part of, and my failings, first as a man, then as a boyfriend, and then again as a husband and family man. Although I don't have a master's or a PhD, I'm going to share with you every lesson I've learned from a life filled with hard knocks. The street corner was my classroom. The hood was my Harvard. And fourteen years of marriage, four kids, a blended family, and a ministry that has allowed me to travel the world have become my laboratory for life.

What I have to offer isn't perfection; it's experience. I've lived through what many of you are experiencing—I had no relationship with my father or my mother; I was abandoned, adopted; I have family members battling drug addictions; I had my own baby mama drama; my wife also had a child when she was very young, which means that we came together with families already in place; I'm trying to balance a career and family; and, like you, I pray to God even though sometimes I struggle to believe that He loves me and knows what in the world He's doing. I battle, like many of you, with faith.

You see, I didn't have any blueprint when I was coming up, any kind of instruction manual on how to be a man. All you have to do is look at any city corner to know that my education was flawed. And so was my behavior. Many of us had either *no* blueprint or a *bad* one—maybe you had to be daddy to a drunk daddy or mama to a mama who was raising you all alone.

There are so many vivid examples from my own flawed upbringing. When I was growing up, I never saw a man who was faithful to his wife. Think about that—not *one*! I was told by my own mother that she did not want me, that she had wanted to abort me. That messed me up real bad! I was confused and hurt by the insecurities of growing up without my pops. Throughout my early childhood, I struggled with not being accepted for a lot of reasons—my adopted family's poverty, my small physical size, my role in the local church choir as a singer and musician, which was definitely not what the hood thought being a man was about.

I am here to tell you that whether you grew up with only a mom, with a drunk daddy, or with a crack-addicted sister, there *is* a blueprint for how to handle everything that life throws at you. And it's not Kirk Franklin's blueprint. It's the blueprint that's been passed from generation to generation, from Moses on down. It's been time-tested. And I know that whenever I went against it, I was slapped down and was lovingly forced to come correct.

Scripture says faith without works is dead. And that's true enough. But I also think faith without truth and honesty is dead. I think faith that takes place only in the church, and then stops at the church doors, is dead. We need a faith that moves out of the pews and becomes the very substance of our lives, one that lives and breathes and becomes part of our body, soul, and spirit. We need to take our faith out of the church and into the realness of everyday life—to the street corners; to the back of the Escalade while Maxwell is playing and we're in the mood but not thinking about the consequences of the day after; to the home where we drink and curse around our kids and expect them to differentiate when it's wrong for them but right for us; to this pseudo-love that sticks around only when you satisfy my needs but when the money, the youth, and the fun run out, I run out with it and take the twenty-year-old secretary with me.

Here is the heartbeat of this book: We have to deal with *reality* if we're going to come up with a blueprint for our lives. And you are definitely going to get slices of reality in this book, a reality that hopefully will set you and those you love on the right road.

If the Obama presidential campaign taught us anything, it's that people need hope. Not canned hope that comes hermetically sealed, but rather the kind of hope that comes from real life, from one person's struggles serving as an example to others. Whatever your political tastes, you have to see that the message of Barack Obama connected with people on a very basic level because his story is full of hope. It's his story, but it's our story as well—daddy from Kenya, mama from Kansas, parents divorced while he was a baby, no contact with dad. The specifics may not parallel ours, but the struggles do. I want my story to be one of hope, not because I've done everything right, but because of the mistakes I've made, the journey I've been on, and how I am striving every day, fighting to correct myself so I won't fall off the path. I am here to put my story—and all my faults and blemishes—on the line. Dirty laundry, even the stuff in the dryer. Because it's your story, too.

I'm letting you know now, the road is going to get a whole lot uglier before it gets better. But that ugliness is there for a purpose. That purpose is to provide you, your spouse, your family, your kids with a spiritual blueprint, one that will help you pass through the ugliness and into hope. If this lost boy forced to be a man can do it, with God's grace, there's hope for everybody. We are all fighting for our lives right now. And I'm right there with you. Together we're going to destroy the walls of frustration and self-doubt, despair, and fear. With hammers in both hands—we'll call them hope and faith—we'll build those walls back up on a solid foundation. The blueprint. God's blueprint.

I believe with all my heart—because I am a living example of this—that despite the tragedies and painful misfortunes that are bound to happen in our lives, some of which we have no control over, God will work out all things for our good. Paul broke it down like this in Romans 8:28: *And we know that all things work together for good to them that love God, to them who are the called according to his purpose.* We will learn together to believe the power of this Scripture. We will learn together to fight the good fight, to run the race set before us without giving up.

I got a great lesson in the power of this Scripture back in the nineties, when I had one of the scariest trials of my life. More than a decade after it happened, I have the advantage of hindsight to see just how much one fateful day changed my path and led me to a blueprint for my life.

It happened in 1996, just eight months after my wedding to Tammy. She was pregnant at the time and I was on the verge of becoming a true family man. But I wasn't really ready for it. I was still immature in a lot of ways; I still carried some of the residue of my single days—the wandering eyes, the single man swag. I wanted to live right, but I had no idea how to go about it. I had no blueprint, no template for the life I wanted. I didn't have any married men around me who modeled what a beautiful, healthy, young, sexy, Christian marriage looked like. That was important to me because I was all too aware of what happens to Christians when they settle into their lives in the church—they lose their sauce. Where in the Bible does it say that when you become born-again, you have to leave your swag at the altar? If you liked fried chicken before you became born-again, you can still like fried chicken afterward. If you liked to salsa dance, you can still salsa dance—though His spirit inside of you may be saying that skirt needs to come down a little bit. It's almost like we get up from the altar, leave the prayer line, and we think God hands us a list of things we now *can't* do. As Christians, I think we should be given a list of what we *can* do.

So I was newly married and primed for some kind of intervention, something to help me figure out how to live this life I wanted but couldn't find. I was in Memphis for a concert, backstage with my crew. I did something that was very much out of character for me: I told the crew that I believed something was going to happen that night that would change our lives. Understand, I'm not one of those prophet types who walks around telling people that God is about to perform a miracle. But on this day I suppose I felt something different. I went out onstage to open the show, which meant I was getting ready to introduce Yolanda Adams. When I went backstage, I was walking toward the dressing room with a friend from the crew. It was dark back there, and there was a large curtain separating the stage from the orchestra pit on the other side of the arena, where apparently there was a small theater. My friend said he turned around to speak to someone, and when he turned back to me, I was gone. He reached through the curtain and saw that the ground disappeared and he freaked out. They turned the lights on and I was down there lying in a puddle of blood. I just missed hitting a huge pipe organ with my head. But I went into a coma with contusions to the brain. They had to call Tammy to travel to Memphis while she was pregnant. The doctors told them that because I landed on the left side of my head, I probably wouldn't be able to perform again, write again, or even speak well. I was in a coma for a total of four days. When I came out of it, the doctors were concerned because I was very hyperactive. My people said, "Okay, he was already hyperactive." Then the doctors warned that when they tried to talk to me, I kind of stuttered. My people said, "Ooookay, he already stuttered." Then the doctors explained that sometimes I'd move real fast, then suddenly slow down. My people said, "He already did that—so he's doing good!" I left the hospital after five days; I had to take it easy at home for a while recuperating, but we were able to resume the tour after about two months.

I believe that God put me through that pain to make me realize that even though I had experienced a certain amount of success in the gospel music world and had achieved some fame, I was nowhere near the kind of man He wanted me to be. A few weeks before that fall, my wife and I had gone out to spend some time together. I went into the closet of the hotel room where we were staying to do some meditating and praying. I felt this great presence and knew it was God's presence there with me. His voice spoke into my heart, telling me how things were going to drastically change for me. It was definitely a prelude to the fall. So when I emerged from that accident I had a sense that it was time for me to grow up, time to put my man hat on. I may not have had the right lessons and models to show me how to be a man, but God was telling me that if I stayed close to Him, He would teach me. The generations of neglect and failure had to stop with me; I couldn't pass it on to my sons. My daddy gave it to me and his daddy gave it to him, but He was letting me know it would stop with me. So that fall turned out to be an enormous help to me. *All things work together for good.*

Let me preach just a little bit. Soul sickness being passed down from generation to generation can happen at any time, to anyone. Even to King David, whose years since he was a youngster were committed to Israel and the Lord. But one day, he let his thoughts wander while he was watching Bathsheba. And thinking those thoughts wasn't enough; this dude went over to her house and slept with a married woman. I know this happens so much now that it doesn't provoke that "Oooh girl" reaction. But this started a saga that later plagued David's family, a saga that started with the murder of Bathsheba's husband, who worked for David. Wow. And then David's first boy, Amnon, picked up where his daddy left off and slept with his half sister Tamar. When his brother Absalom found out what Amnon had done, he took him out—that's right, he killed his own brother. Once ignited, this story continued like an episode of *Desperate Housewives*—incest, murder, war, jealousy, spite—all the way down to Solomon, another one of David's many sons, who also had a serious woman problem, thus continuing the messed-up-family drama.

But the beautiful thing about *your* life is that you have a blueprint of what *not* to do, how *not* to live your life. All David had was David. And Solomon had to deal with the jacked-up legacy and reputations of his father, David, and his brothers Absalom and Amnon. So begin following the blueprint by forgiving the Davids in your past. Forgive your daddy. Forgive your mama. Forgive your former pastor. You know why? They've suffered enough for their sins. And you know what? You are here; and you have the opportunity to move ahead, to pass a fresh outlook to your children, and their children. To give them a new blueprint.

Two of the biggest scourges on the African-American community today are the high divorce rate and the high number of single-parent families (in which the parent is most likely a woman). We all know that many factors contribute to the failure of marriage and the fragility of African-American families today. We could spend hours debating the effects of slavery, economics, and drugs in communities of color. (And I believe each of these has played a significant part in our getting here.) But what about all the stories of black men during the Depression, Jim Crow, and segregation who worked heroically to provide for their families at any cost? The values that were taught in those homes created a level of self-respect and pride that we can *still* see in our grandparents, the elders of our Tribe. Those values *must* be part of our blueprint.

Hope I haven't bored you yet. In this book, I'm going to challenge you to do something difficult on a regular basis. I want you to talk to God. I want you to do it because He is your Father, because He is your friend. But I don't want you to do it in some churchy, religious way. No, I want you to talk to Him like He's your brother, your counselor, your boy, your pops. I want you to have a real conversation with Him. I want you to tell Him that you're mad, that you're scared, or whatever it is—don't be afraid to be real. I want you to have an honest conversation with the Lord right now about the anger and hurt that you have, about the fact that you're tired. Now. Let Him hear you talk, let Him hear you scream; holler if you want. Don't be afraid to be you; He made you unique. Stop trying to be super-spiritual and just be real.

And I want you to hear God telling you that He is wiping your slate clean. That you are qualified. That you can stop being afraid. I don't care how many women your daddy had, *you* can be faithful. I don't care how many men your mother was with, *you* can be faithful. It can work. You can keep your job. Your job can work. You can stay off alcohol. You can stay out of the club. You don't need those drugs. You don't need to be afraid. Your despair will end. You can close up your legs. You can move into the faith.

And keep saying, "I'm qualified," until you believe it.

No matter how many conversations it takes with your Father, "I'm qualified. I'm qualified."

No matter what life presents you with, "I'm qualified. I can move into the faith. I'm a runner. I *am* qualified."

Now all you need is the blueprint.

In each of the following chapters, we will undertake the process of constructing your blueprint, adding all the various aspects of your life, taking away the things that are harming you (weeds), so that the final result will be as strong and sturdy a structure as your life could possibly be, a building that any one of us would love to call home.

THE BLUEPRINT

Chapter One

MOVIN' ON UP

When I was a kid, one of my favorite ways to pass time was to sit on the orange shag carpet in the house of my great-aunt Gertrude, the woman who adopted me, and watch television. There were two shows in particular that I really looked forward to, *The Jeffersons* and *Good Times*. I'm sure you remember them. George Jefferson was owner of a dry-cleaning business that had achieved enough success for him to move his family to that "deluxe apartment" in Manhattan. I can still hear that theme music in my head, talking about "movin' on up." And then there were James and Florida Evans on *Good Times*. Life hadn't been so kind to them; they were still stuck in the projects in Chicago. "Scratching and surviving," as the theme song said. I'm sure one of the main reasons I got excited about these shows, even at the tender age of seven or eight, was the chance to see black people on TV. I would sit there under our new ceiling fan in the front of the house, getting some relief from the Texas heat, and watch George swagger around the TV, and then watch James broil as his kids—mainly J.J.—got the family stuck in yet another crazy predicament.

What neither show ever explained was how George managed to make his way out of the ghetto while James didn't. How, for instance, did George finance his business dreams? Did he, as a black man, *really* get a small business loan in the seventies to open a dry cleaner in the ghetto? How often did he and Weezy stay up late at night praying over their bills? Did they have marital problems due to the stress of raising a son—and, if so, how did they deal with those problems? Did George have to cancel date nights because of overtime at the office?

All the show gave us was George and Louise moving in and adjusting (or trying to adjust) to their new life. But what about the valleys in their old one? What did the Jeffersons do right that the Evanses didn't?

One thing that did stand out to me as a little boy was the fact that George had money and influence, whereas James didn't. James didn't have a voice and he seemed to be mad all the time. James must have been so frustrated and bitter about his situation, that he had no one willing to help him, no one close enough to offer winning advice. (Maybe everyone was just too afraid to risk the wrath of J.J.'s daddy—and James could conjure some serious wrath.) Maybe never getting a break finally made James stop dreaming. Maybe he simply gave up trying to live and just started existing. That is a state way too many of us are familiar with.

But I think the greatest difference between George and James was that one had a blueprint and the other one didn't. One had a plan to see his way out, the other didn't.

When I reflect on my life and the lives of others like me, I see that too often we live with constant frustration and bitterness, with no sense of preparation or moral direction. No guidelines to help us. We have no plans to see our way out of our predicaments. A great sense of disenfranchisement has been created by our lack of attention to education, true manhood, sex, and race—as well as by popular but unbiblical theology. Slam-dunking a ball, spitting a fresh "sixteen bars" on the mike (or rapping, for you civilians), placing career over family, having lots of ladies' phone numbers in the BlackBerry—these are our images of manhood. Hips, lips, low-cut jeans, gold diggers, *Flavor of Love* contestants embarrassing themselves for the chance to give themselves to men they barely know—these are our images of beautiful women. Murder in the streets, platinum grills (or teeth, stay with me!), high dropout and pregnancy rates, no respect for the adults in their lives—these are all-too-real images of our gifted but abandoned children. Meanwhile, celebrities, the *Enquirer*, television, pop music, half-hearted politicians, and disconnected churches have become our (broken) foundations.

If that's what we have to build our lives on, no wonder everything we've come to trust in has begun to show cracks. Or even to have fallen apart completely. It's unfair to the greatness inside every man, woman, boy, and girl to try to understand the purpose for the gift of life—a gift God has given each of us—without a blueprint.

I didn't find my true blueprint until I was in my late twenties. And it came largely through my relationship with a brilliant man, my pastor Tony Evans. That's why I'm such a strong advocate for mentoring, having men speaking to the lives of men, and women with a purpose speaking to the lives of women. I have a nine-year-old boy who is a source of endless fascination for me because most everything about him is a result of what I've poured into him. That's just amazing to me because it's so different from what I had at his age. Everything I've become has been the result of painful lessons over a long period of time. But my little boy is getting a lot of the lessons without the bumps.

There have been other men who I thought were going to be the mentors that I needed, but most of them eventually imparted bad lessons, the wrong messages. But Tony Evans for me modeled exactly the life I wanted to live and the man I wanted to become. When you look under his carpet, you don't see chicks' phone numbers, condoms, money stashed away in Swiss accounts. He's been married to the same woman for decades. He doesn't have a lot of swag or flavor. In other words, Tony ain't fresh. But I would trade all of that to have some of the solidness he has. He's got that vital stuff, the meat you need on your bones when the storms of life come blowing your way. Spending time with Tony enabled me to start developing the plans to the blueprint of my life.

I believe with all my heart, because I am a living example of this, that despite the tragedies and painful misfortunes that have happened in our lives, some of which we have no control over, God will work all things out for our good. Romans 8:28 is my joint, y'all! I love this one. Let's read it again.

And we know that all things work together for good to them that love God, to them who are the called according to his purpose.

When you read it, take a close look at the word "all." Did you read that? Again, slowly . . . *all*. Does that mean that God will even take my mistakes and use them for something great? *All*. Can He take this abuse or the lump I've had in the center of my chest since I buried my son? *All*. What about this economy? The plant closing—come on, Kirk, that doesn't make sense! *All*.

Several years ago, I worked with John Amos, the actor who played James Evans on *Good Times*. I asked him why he left the show without even finishing the season. He said he left because he grew tired of the images the show constantly presented of black people. Basically, and perhaps ironically, trouble came to the set because James was *not* having a good time.

Are you tired of compromising? Of living and working and acting out your life in ways that don't bring you contentment and personal satisfaction? Is your image and that of those around you not looking the way you want it to? Do you feel like it just won't get any better? It's never too late to start over, to turn the channel, to flip the page. On one channel you may be "keeping your head above water, making a way if you can," but there's another that will help you move on up to all that God has in store for you. *Eye has not seen; nor ear heard, nor have entered into the heart of man the things which God has prepared for those who love Him* (1 Corinthians 2:9). It's a new day, filled with new grace. So change that channel!

George and Weezy, don't get too comfortable, baby—you've got company!

Chapter Two

THE ULTIMATE BLUEPRINT

Imagine the crew at a construction site where a building is being erected. Cement trucks arrive. Steel beams are delivered. Miles of electrical wires wait to be installed. All crew members are in place, anxious to get to work. But they get no signal to break ground. Something's holding up the work, delaying the start of construction. After waiting what seems an eternity, one of the workers gets frustrated with the waiting and goes to the foreman.

"What's the problem?" he asks.

"No one can find the blueprint!" comes the reply.

So they wait. And frustration builds . . . and builds . . . and builds. And the crew loses patience. Eventually, it becomes too much. They reach their limit. They want action and they want it *now*. So finally they decide to strike out to do their own thing, *to build without a blueprint*.

And why not? They are, after all, professionals; they're more than qualified to construct the building. If they weren't, they wouldn't have been hired in the first place. And being professionals, this isn't their first building. Not by a long shot. They work at construction sites almost every day. This gig is how they pay their bills. Given such experience, they think, this job will be easy—*even without a blueprint.*

But they are wrong.

After a few days of working without a master plan, of relying on their own experiences rather than on the wisdom of a master designer, confusion and disorder kick in. Every member of the crew does what is right in his own eyes. Windows appear where doors should be. The toilets all end up on the roof. The air-conditioning goes in backward—settings for heat make things colder and those for cold make them hotter. City inspectors can't approve the job because nobody plans for fire exits. The crew members assume they can construct the building on their own, without a blueprint; in the end, though, they build a catastrophe, an architectural disaster.

When folks decide to ignore the instruction manual that tells them how to live according to the plan for which they were created, to stop communicating altogether with life's architect, or to adjust things on the fly with no concern for the architect's blueprint, they void their warranties. After all, warranties only cover original parts used according to plan; they cover things used in the way they were intended to be used. They *don't* cover after-market features, adjustments made against the master plan. Put 22s on your Benz and the wheels are no longer covered.

Now we take *God's* creation and add after-market changes. We tinker with values. We tamper with right and wrong. We re-arrange things according to *our* tastes, not according to the blueprint; by *our* likes, not by the book. And when things don't work right, we wonder why.

We void the warranty. *We* ignore the manufacturer's specs. *We* do what is right in *our* eyes. And when things go wrong, we wonder why, sometimes even asking, "Where is God?" We add spoilers and custom paint jobs, *but he doesn't cover after-market features.*

So we try to build life on *our* terms. We don't use God's instruction manual for our lives. We proceed according to our own understanding. And wars continue; more than that, they multiply. The rich get richer; the poor get poorer. Politicians can't keep their promises.

Left to our own understanding, we no longer see what's wrong. We don't want to offend anyone, so the standard keeps changing. We ask God to help us when we face trouble, but to leave us alone when all is well. "I'm cool right now, God, so please let a brother have his space." The less gospel we hear, the more hatred and oppression we see. It can't be a coincidence that the less we hear God, the more we see ungodliness.

A construction crew might be qualified to construct a building, but they still need a blueprint.

As for you and me, science can't provide our blueprint. It can help us better understand God's world, but it can't be the foundation we stand on. Neither philosophy nor religion can provide our blueprint. These never-ending quests for knowledge and understanding are, well, *never ending.* So they can help us better understand ourselves, but they can't give us a complete and final picture of ourselves. To understand our world, ourselves, how to live (rather than just survive)—for that, we need to pursue the world's architect, its Master Planner. No one else can tell me why I am here and what I am to do with the time I have. If you void your warranty, you create a world divided, a humanity in turmoil.

Let's get started on helping you figure out what your own personal blueprint looks like, what the master plan is for you.

Embrace the non-sexies.
Out of all the lessons in this book, this one just may be the most crucial. It is your attention to the details of your life, your commitment to the non-sexy things, the non-celebrated things, that will give your life meaning and substance. When we see the public you shining, we will know it's because you did the private work.

This message came to me loud and clear a few years back when I was on tour with Donnie McClurkin and Yolanda Adams. We had a day off and Donnie and Yolanda flew out of town to do a cameo in a movie. Donnie and Yolanda have not tried to knock on Hollywood's doors nearly as much as I have over the last several years. I've done pilots, plays, had movie scripts, movie offers, but nothing has come to pass. Yet it was Donnie and Yolanda who got the call to do a cameo in this movie on our off day. There was even a private jet sent to bring them to the set. As for me, I was catching a plane back home to be with the kids. I remember I was giving my son Caziah a bath; while I was washing him it crossed my mind that Donnie and Yolanda were doing what I would have loved to be doing. I felt really frustrated. "Man, they're on a movie set and here I am at home giving a five-year-old a bath!" But as soon as I said that, God's voice spoke to my heart and said, *You're doing exactly what I want you to do. This is the most important thing you could be doing right now.*

We naturally don't think like that. I was thinking that my dudes were shooting cameos in a movie and I'm leaning over a bathtub with a five-year-old. But I came to realize that those little things are what make you powerful when you stand up in front of people. It's not getting off the stage and flying somewhere to do an interview or be in a movie. I'm proud for my friends, so this isn't about hating, but I'm learning that's not the stuff that makes you powerful, that gives you essence, that gives you substance. You can see this very clearly with our actors. When we talk about why certain actors rise to the A-list, with a bit of investigation we find out they studied, they trained, they did the work. When Hilary Swank did the movie *Amelia*, she studied everything about Amelia Earhart, even getting her walk down. Or when we watch Jamie Foxx in *Booty Call* and then watch him in *Ray*, we can see the difference, that he started doing the work. It's obvious there was work done before the cameras were even turned on. Sometimes in our lives we want to show up when the cameras are on, but we don't want to do the work before. You can even go through college and not do the work. You can get a master's degree and not do the work. You can get a PhD but not have internalized the work. We're too often in pursuit of the sheepskin, the paper, without internalizing the work.

How do you figure out what the work is in your own life? You embrace the things you realize are divinely there. These are the non-sexies. *What are the things in my life that cannot give me applause, can't bring me bonuses, that can't always return back what I give?* Whatever they are, those are the things you need to be committed to. This is the way we fight against the selfishness, the shallowness of our lives. When we do for somebody because they can do something for us, that's not getting into the depth of who we are. Too many of the things in our lives have conditions. We love and we give and we serve and we work, but they all have conditions. It's all about what we're going to get back in return. But if we start to make decisions and find those areas in our lives that have no conditions, and then give our time and money and hearts, we will start to transform who we are at a very deep level. A level that will have long-lasting effects on our lives.

What are the sexies? You know what they are. The sexies are the spontaneous, the off-the-cuff, the off-the-hook. *It's 2 o'clock in the morning, let's run down to the club. . . . Let me give some*

*money to that charity and get a tax credit. . . . Ooh, check out the
new BMWs; I'm working more overtime so I can get me one of those!*
All of that doesn't take any discipline; you're just moving, running on your emotions. You can't trust emotions—and they
were never meant to be trusted. Emotions were never meant to
be the engine; emotions were always the caboose.

You want to know the kind of people I want to be around?
The mother who cares for a child who is disabled. The husband
who stays committed to his dying wife's bedside. The person
who volunteers his nights down at the homeless shelter. Those
are the people with the most peace and soberness, the most character. They are doing jobs that are not sexy. Jobs that the child
or the wife or the homeless could applaud, but it's an applause
only heaven can give. I want to ask them, *How do you do that?*
When you can find the substance in you that allows you to do
things like that, you can handle losing your job, you can handle
the economy bugging out, you can handle all the things that are
driving us crazy right now.

I saw a commercial recently that blew my mind. It was for
people who are on antidepressants; it said three out of seven
people, or something like that, who are on antidepressants still
sometimes suffer from depression. So this commercial was for a
new pill that they had come up with that you would take in ad-
dition to the antidepression pill! It was one of those commercials
where the guy goes on reading the horrible side effects for like
five minutes, when he's mumbling real fast in a lower voice . . .
*"This pill may cause insomnia, heart disease, infertility, mumble,
mumble, mumble . . ."* I was saying to myself, *I got a pill I can tell
you about that brought a serious change to my life!* Even though
medication has its place, when I thought I would have to get on
some type of medication because I thought I was crazy, I surren-
dered my life to the Lord. It was not even about religion; it was
more about a relationship. I got out of me and it changed every-

thing about my life. I didn't feel all those things I felt before—depression, fear, anxiety, selfishness. Because when you're feeling those things, you start all your sentences with "I." *What am I going to do?* Whenever everything starts with "I," then you're in trouble. I'm not saying self-preservation is not important, but it's not *the* most important thing. I hope you're feeling me!

You know how when you meet older black people who were around when things were very hard for black folks in this country, they still seem like they somehow have hope and strength? That's because their hope was never in those materialistic, selfish, superficial things in the first place. You see the footage of them being sprayed by the police with water hoses, having dogs attacking them, and you wonder, *How did they live through that?* Somehow we seemed to be stronger then, didn't we? We have bought into the messages from the TV, from the commercials; we have bought into the medication, the worldly things, as if we didn't hear the rest of the commercial. . . . *"This job promotion . . . this affair . . . this negative attitude . . . may cause insomnia, heart disease, infertility, mumble, mumble, mumble . . ."*

Examine the fruit.

Some of you might be tempted to ask, *How do I know if I'm working with the right blueprint, the one that will relieve me from the despair?* Well, let me see if I can make it clearer. If someone goes to the same soul food shack all their lives, then one Sunday someone invites them to a five-star restaurant, they will immediately start noticing all the differences. The plates are different, the fork is heavier than the plastic they are used to, the ambience is different, the presentation is different. When you cut into the steak, it's like it just falls off the bone. And when you put it into your mouth, it feels like it dissolves on your tongue. Once you taste that, nobody can ever tell you there's no difference. I'm not saying you won't ever like or appreciate Joe's Rib Shack again, but you won't say Joe's Rib Shack is the best thing in the world you've ever tasted because you've been introduced to something greater.

When you meet people and their lives have fruit, when their lives are filled with the non-sexies, it's very obvious they're doing something right. You see it in their homes, you see it in their children, you see it in their careers, you see it in the way they talk, in their state of mind, how they think. In other words, you can tell if it's a good blueprint by examining the fruit. If it's right, it has an unmistakable glow, one that makes you look on in admiration and amazement. But you have to be careful. You can be so hungry for the attention that you overlook the stuff that you know isn't right. You go off in the wrong direction. Because of how you view yourself, you don't take the time to think, *You know what, this is not what I deserve*. That's a trap that we all have fallen into at one time or another. We have to pay attention to what our souls are trying to tell us as we attempt to walk the right path. If the fruit doesn't look right and smell right, keep stepping.

Not even Kobe can do it alone.

It is possible that these changes you begin to make within yourself won't be warmly embraced or understood by the people who are close to you. In this case, you have to let everybody know how they're going to benefit from a better you. You have to reinforce what everybody's going to get from it. And that's how it should be—everybody around you *should* be benefiting. If you're the only one becoming better because of you, then you're not becoming better, you're becoming selfish. No matter how good Kobe is, he can't win on his own. He has to have all the other players around him, the entire team, working in sync if he's going to achieve his goals and win championships. When he tries to do it by himself, which happened early in his career, he always came up short. If your changes are going to affect the people around you, maybe make them feel belittled or alienated, you have to change the approach. You need your entire team with you, all working together in sync. Even Scripture says, *With loving kindness I have drawn thee* (Jeremiah 31:3).

I'm always intrigued when I watch the awards shows because it seems that the more successful someone is, the more people they need to thank. They go up there onstage and start giving their speech, all the time watching that clock tick away, and many of the great ones go over their time and the director has to start the music. Because the true winners know they didn't get there by themselves.

I can remember a period in my life when my wife, Tammy, acted as a particularly crucial member of my team. It was 2001 and I can recall it like it happened yesterday. Nothing seemed to be going right for me at the time. There were quite a few projects that looked like they were just about to jump off, but none of them actually worked out. We were sitting in the car in a parking lot and I was doing a lot of whining and complaining about how things weren't working out for me. My wife listened for a while, then she said, "I hear you, but what are you going to do about it?" She didn't say it in a belittling way that challenged my manhood or anything. But I got the message loud and clear. She was saying that I needed to man up, that she was looking for me to be the leader of the family. I was taken aback that she could see that in me at that moment. But I got the message. And I was so grateful that I had somebody like her on my team.

But I know getting your team in sync isn't always as easy as it sounds. Someone recently asked me how she could help her friend, a woman whose husband attends the same church that she attends. The woman is not growing at this church; she feels spiritually stunted there and wants to go elsewhere to deepen her relationship with the Lord. But she has a problem: Her husband likes the church and doesn't want to leave. He has some homies there, the pastor is his golf partner, and he's comfortable. You know how we men are—we become creatures of habit. I can easily see his perspective: *Leave me alone; you wanted me to go to church, and here I am.* But she's dying in that church and desperately needs to go somewhere else, though she doesn't want to make the change alone. She wants her partner along with her. She wants the two of them to move in sync. I told the woman that this is what her friend needs to say to her husband:

Baby, you are my man and I am here to help you become the greatest man you can be. You are so important to me and important to this home. I want to be everything God put in me to be for you because you deserve that. But where we are right now, I am not able to maximize who I am for you. I am not able to give you my best because I'm not learning my best. I am dying here and I don't want to do that because you deserve better than that. I want you to have the best wife in the world.

Now he has to be either dumb or flat-out ignorant (let me rephrase: ig'nant) to hear that and not respond to it! As a man, if my wife said that to me, touching all my man buttons and telling me how I'm going to benefit, I would be about ready to run through a wall for her (as I throw up the peace sign on my way out of the church!).

This is your life—not a step program.

Before I go on and talk about all the elements of your blueprint in the rest of the chapters, let me say this: This program is a life-long journey, not a step program. I think the most destructive thing we have done to people is we have given them steps. But the kind of meaningful change I'm seeking for you does not come in steps. Everybody wants to know, *What do I need to do?* The quick boom boom boom. But nothing good is made in the boom boom boom. You don't make good love in the boom boom boom; maybe a quickie, but not good love. You don't make a good home in the boom boom boom. You don't make a good career in the boom boom boom. You don't make a good meal in the boom boom boom. Everything that has been good to us as human beings was created over time. And that's why the steps are not working. As I said before, they're offering a pill to help people on a pill! Clearly, this society's way to make people happy is not working. I understand that people want their change quick. But that's not the way it should work if it's going to be long lasting. You get on the journey and what happens is the things you're wrestling with this year won't be the things you're wrestling with next year.

So stay with me here and hopefully you will discover the elements of the journey that God has divinely inspired for you.

Chapter Three

Upon This Rock

I t's fascinating to me as I get older to recognize how much of the way we are can be directly connected to things that happened to us when we were children. This gets even clearer when we try to become emotionally and spiritually healthy as adults. I had one of these revelations when I entered my thirties and started to struggle a lot with anxiety. It was this general sense of fear that I just couldn't understand. Sometimes it was fear of flying, sometimes it was elevators, sometimes it was death. Sometimes I couldn't even point to a particular reason; I'd be by myself somewhere and just be afraid. But the healthier I became spiritually, the more I learned to stop and ask myself, *Okay, what are you afraid of right now?* And then I would assess and say, *Right, there's nothing happening right now; nothing to be afraid of.* But one day I thought back to my childhood and it hit me: When I was growing up, I was always afraid. It just followed me into adulthood.

Now that I'm an adult and a father, when I look back on my childhood I can understand why I was always so afraid and anxious. I was abandoned as a baby. My mother was only fifteen and couldn't take care of me and my daddy just took off, so my moms and pops weren't in my life. When I was four I was adopted by my great-aunt Gertrude, my grandmother's sister, so my mama was in and out of my life because she still had a relationship with Gertrude. She would promise to pick me up, but most of the time she didn't. Gertrude stayed constantly mad at me because as I got older I was not living up to her expectations. So I would wake up never knowing what my day was going to be. I contrast that with my kids now—we've been through recessions, wars, terror attacks, anthrax, buildings blowing up and falling down, and I got two little Buppie black kids who haven't lost a night of sleep yet. Because their worlds are not our worlds. And that's how it should be. But when I was coming up, I started out with a terribly unhealthy and contaminated foundation, and the instability and unsteadiness naturally extended straight into adulthood. If our foundation is shaky, no amount of money and fame is going to make it solid. That sturdiness and strength only comes by putting in that private work.

The most important thing that Gertrude did for me was she introduced me to Jesus. She was a church woman to the core, even at home. Our home life looked just like what I saw at church. There was no hypocrisy in our dilapidated old house. When she was washing dishes or making cobbler, Gertrude would be singing gospel songs. She was always singing and praying. She didn't drink; she didn't cuss—later on, I did enough for the both of us!

The good days for me stopped at about age twelve. That's when my foundation really got weak and foul. Gertrude didn't seem to understand that I couldn't remain a little boy forever. When I approached my teen years, she sort of cut me off. She didn't know how to deal with a boy going through puberty and all the changes that come with it. I was no longer little Kirk; now

I wanted to talk to girls on the phone. In her eyes I became a demon child. If I got in trouble at school, by the time I got home the whole block would know. I grew up not feeling covered, protected. My blueprint was fear; my blueprint was insecurity; my blueprint was "they'll like you if you perform"; my blueprint was loneliness; my blueprint was sex. And my blueprint was Jesus. Whatever spiritual seed that was placed inside of me as a little boy never seemed to leave me. I always had a sense of a pull, even when I was getting high and clubbing and being promiscuous. I always lived with an awareness that there was something greater, something bigger than me. But it would be a while before I was ready for it.

She put Jesus in my life, but the years with Gertrude left their mark. She had a way of reminding me when I wasn't wanted. It seemed I was *always* in trouble. One time she even called me a bastard. Gertrude was very careful with the words she used, so she meant it in the truest sense of the word, not as just a random cuss (and I already told you that Gertrude didn't cuss). I *was* a bastard, but I didn't want to hear anybody calling me that. It hurt. Most of the things I did, at least the things she knew about, was just me being a growing boy. I liked talking to girls on the phone; I was the only child in the house, so the phone was my life. In my neighborhood, everybody was older than me so I didn't have many kids to play with. I would come home from school and she'd have taken all the phones out of the jacks. That was her way of getting back at me for talking.

Now, there were things I was doing away from the house and Gertrude that were not right, like smoking, drinking, and being very promiscuous at a very young age. We were eleven and twelve and being sexual—and I mean *sexual*. Not touching it or tickling it; I mean doin' it. That was incredibly destructive because of what sex became for me. Sex became how I interpreted love. With no supervision, no reinforcing love, no reaffirming values,

I found these things in girls because they were also looking for something they didn't have. It's very interesting how you become magnets for people just like you. Whoever you are, however you are, you become a magnet for that.

When I was thirteen Gertrude got mad at me on Thanksgiving and packed up all my stuff. It was about bad grades or something like that. She sent me over to my mother's house. But my mother didn't want me there either—and I overheard her telling Gertrude that she regretted not aborting me like she wanted to. So that same night I was sent back to Gertrude. Four years later, I came home on Valentine's Day and Gertrude had all my stuff packed up again. She said she was tired of me being on the phone all the time calling these little girls. I had to go live with a friend for about a month before she let me back in the house. When Gertrude got remarried when I was thirteen and suddenly there was a man in the house, I didn't know whether he was going to like me and feared that they might send me away. So I was raised with an uncertainty about even having a home. "Insecure" doesn't begin to describe it. Outside the house things weren't much better. I was not liked by the other kids because I was that little piano-playing Negro. I didn't have much swag because I lived with this old woman who made my clothes. When I asked her for a Jheri curl, because *everybody* had a Jheri curl, she said that she could do it herself. But she gave me those big bouncy curls, with the pink rollers, where you could still see the parts in my hair. So I looked like Big Perm in the movie *Friday*. Sometimes I wanted to break down like Florida Evans and just scream, "D*mn, d*mn, d*mn!"

Just to show how far these early insecurities can extend into adulthood if they aren't corrected, the first concert of mine that Tammy—then my fiancée—went to was at a big theater in Oakland called the Paramount, and the place was sold out. As she tells the story, after the show I kept asking her, "How did I do?"

At the time, she said to herself, "This man is so arrogant! He saw all those people out there screaming." But after we were married she realized that I was actually serious; I was so insecure that I really wanted to know. But that was the blueprint for insecurity, still all wobbly on top of my shaky foundation.

I will never forget this one incident with Gertrude that kind of summarized my childhood. I was thirteen or fourteen and we were in the kitchen. She was mad, again, about something I had done. What I said to her was very wise for me at that age, very mature. I said, "You never tell me nothing good about myself! If I play [music] in church and do things like that, you never tell me anything good. But if I do something bad, everybody know about it." She looked at me and said, "Boy, you just want somebody to praise you." And she was right! I just needed somebody to praise me. We all do. Especially from those who mold us. It kills me even as I write this, that she couldn't give me that.

A few years ago I did an interview on the *Oprah Winfrey Show* during which I shared my testimony about my past with pornography. Basically I struggled with a pornography addiction that was all wrapped up in my confusion that sex was love—a confusion that was spawned when I was a young boy. The reaction to that interview has been fascinating to me, particularly the stark difference between the reaction of the black community and the reaction of the white community. The only reason the Oprah people knew about my story was because I had been talking about it for three years before that, on the cover of Christian magazines and all over the Christian media. But outside of the Christian media it wasn't well known. After the Oprah show, some reactions in the black community killed me. I even had big-time celebrities, I mean *real* big, say to me, "Why did you do that? Man, don't you *ever* put your business out there like that again!" Mind you, I love my people. But we are definitely a proud race of people that does not like telling our stuff. The Bible says, *Pride cometh before the fall.* But the way my white and Hispanic Christian friends treated me, you would have thought I was Billy Graham. They really bigged me up. Despite the reaction of some of these black celebrities, I have a lot of black men and women still come up to me and say I saved their marriage. I've had some hard, cornrow-wearing Negroes, straight out the joint with tattoos all up and down their necks, come up and tell me, "N*gga, what you did really helped me."

It all made me realize how uncomfortable we are with people telling on themselves, revealing painful things. We're much more comfortable when we see people get busted for something, because then it's easier to disconnect. But when I, on my own terms, with no hidden agenda, come forward and say these things, it makes the viewer have to think about his own stuff. But I truly think that's why I'm alive. I'm here for no other reason but to be a walking testimony. And sometimes you're going to get some flack for that.

My point is, even with all of that contamination in your foundation, all that foulness and insecurity in your early life, all those weak and destructive blueprints that were handed to you, it's not too late for you to make it. I'm living proof of that. No matter your background, your family circumstances, the poverty of your parents, it is still possible for you to transform all of that into stunning success. In my mind, that is only because of God's wisdom in constructing a world that gives us many chances to get it right. Please come with me as we ponder all the ways that He has made it possible for you to turn this thing around. Let us consider the brilliance of the work done by the Master Planner.

He evens the playing field.
Life has always been friendlier to the haves, brutal to the have-nots. Throughout history, kingdoms and their rulers have abused

and enslaved those who were weaker, less educated, or whose resources didn't allow them to bribe their way out of the tyranny of wicked leaders.

Yes, some of these folks claimed to be men and women of God and excused their tyranny by claiming to do his work. But those of us who have been on both sides of religion and wealth understand that a title is only as good as the heart behind it. A so-called Christian with a wicked heart is like a lamp with no lightbulb. (*Sorry, Constantine, you, too!*)

Even in modern America, we still see communities that resemble third world countries. Communities where the rich still get richer and the poor get what they've always gotten. Nothing. But the God factor changes things. If I live in a world that bases my value on what I have, I live without hope. If I wasn't born into money, if my name doesn't come with influence and my surroundings don't show up on society's radar, I am one of a forgotten people—those who become second- and third-generation dropouts, low-income dwellers, a people continually frustrated by a life that seems unfair and cruel.

My hope lies not in hearing one more motivational message or in singing one more motivational song. It lies in the truth that my Creator bases my value not on my house, not on my neighborhood, not on my economic status. God values me no less than He values the suburban family with three cars, a pool, and a 401(k). I find strength in His unsurpassable love for me and in the knowledge that the riches of His kingdom outweigh my circumstances—how I was raised, what the government won't do, what my troubles happen to be, and anything else you want to put in the blank.

Our grandparents got along fine without pain pills and depression medicine because their hope and joy were found not in *things* but in the promise that God loved them regardless of what they didn't have, that they were just as precious to Him as those who had more stuff or apparently better circumstances. And they believed that promise because the maker of heaven and earth made it, because He revealed it in His blueprint.

So even if your mom was a crackhead, you have purpose. Even if your father is in prison, you have purpose. Even if you never achieve what we call the "American Dream," you have purpose; you are *not* a mistake. You aren't getting this from some fancy guy in a three-piece suit or someone with a Harvard degree. You are hearing it from someone who tasted dirt just like you did, but who came out on the other side, and who is now in a position to tell you how you can make it.

The world respects power. If you don't have it, the world leaves you behind. But God respects those who choose Him over this world. And He is the equalizer. In *His* court, Ted Turner, Donald Trump, Steve Jobs—they are no more important than Ned the wino, Marcus the convict, David the adulterer, or Kirk the ex–porn addict. Here's hope for the hopeless, strength for the weak, and caution to the powerful: God is no respecter of persons; before Him, we're all the same.

He brings order to the confusion.

Living in a world filled daily with wickedness, tragedy, global threats, hatred, and death, it is tempting to conclude either that God doesn't exist or that, if He does, He is not all-knowing and all-powerful as Christians believe. Because if He was all-knowing and all-powerful, why would He allow such things? This "why" question has long troubled—and probably always will trouble— both believers and non-believers alike. No matter how profound our theological defense of God's sovereignty, we will never satisfy everyone with our response to it.

But if we step into the undercurrent of faith, we may be surprised to see the lines beginning to come together on life's hard issues. We may begin to see how one person's tragedy opens another person's eyes to see God's plan being worked out for the good of all concerned. Or how a prison sentence ultimately saves a man whose life had been spiraling out of control. Or how a teenager's pregnancy teaches one family not to be consumed more with career than with home. Or how God's mysterious ways, however hard and painful they seem, make us wiser, stronger, and better in the end.

Why do bad things happen to good people? I don't know. But when I look through the lens of God's love letters and promises, I see the pieces of life's puzzles come together. And one important thing we should never forget: When God created us, He gave us freedom to choose. Wanting us to choose to love Him, God allows us the choice of whether to do so. We make our choices and we reap the rewards or pay the consequences.

So it makes sense that when a person chooses to do wrong, that choice will have effects that will be long felt. Generations may feel that choice. Nations may feel that choice. And ultimately the whole world may feel it. To me, that makes sense; it also shows how important it is for us to be careful what we choose.

If I can trust Him with all the hell and horrible things in my life—things that made sense in the end—you can, too.

He sets the bar.

As I write this, I am looking at the cover of an issue of *Time* magazine that discusses the increase of infidelity in marriage. The governor of South Carolina has been caught in an extramarital affair, one of many high-profile men whose extramarital relationships have recently been exposed. A popular former football player, a married man with four sons, was recently found murdered with his mistress. Over the last several months, some well-known Christian leaders have also been exposed as being unfaithful to their wives. By the time this book is released, more men and women will find themselves the subjects of tabloid discussions of adultery and secret relationships.

As Wall Street tries to recover from the fallout of recession, schemes have come to light within the financial sector that have ruined the lives of millions of Americans. Financier Bernard Madoff was sentenced to 150 years in prison for lying and mismanaging millions of dollars, leaving many good and honest people with no retirement, bankrupt, broke and in debt.

Whether we're talking about adultery or theft, I'd like to raise an honest question: *Who is to say that these things are wrong?* In a society that wants to quietly get rid of everything resembling God, why do we still continue to use His standards for measuring right and wrong? Why is lying wrong? Why is murder wrong? Why is jealousy wrong? How do we know these things are wrong?

They are wrong because they hurt us and they hurt others. They move us away from God's image, rather than toward it. God gave us the gift of life, and these things cheapen that gift. They damage our humanity. The toddler who has never had an ethics lesson but still struggles with hiding the truth about what really happened to that broken picture frame in the family room, the little girl who knows a certain touch by an older man is not appropriate and begins to cry—both were wired to know right from wrong without being taught the difference. God wired us that way and placed within us a standard, *His* standard.

Some argue that our knowledge of right and wrong comes from our environment. But children from different environments share the same fundamental knowledge of right and wrong. So a child in the most rural part of Indonesia doesn't need to consult with a child in the desert plains of Rwanda for both of them to know that it's wrong to throw rocks at their baby sisters or sneak and play Uncle Mufasa's drums.

Whether you are Muslim, Jewish, or Baptist, you speak a global language about how people should be treated. When Iranians believed their votes were not counted fairly in their last presidential election, they took to the streets to speak against what they know is unjust and wrong. The international community stood along with them as they watched "Neda" lying dead in the street from a gunshot wound.

Why did the whole planet feel pain and sorrow after September 11? We all knew in the inner parts of our being that the murder of innocent people in the two towers was a crime not just against a single country, but against humanity. We saw people all across the planet united, standing together against evil. And those few who brought the towers down were seen as murdering thugs—not just by a few, but by the overwhelming majority of people on the planet.

God created the standard. The bar has been set. But God has given us freedom. And foreseeing all things, God has always known that each man would choose to believe what is right in his own eyes. So a terrorist can choose to fly a plane into a building, killing everyone on the plane and in the building, and do so believing that his "god" will honor his "good" work. And an elected official can rationalize having sexual relationships outside his marriage, hurting not only his wife but also his children and his children's children.

What if God didn't set a standard beyond that of a murdering terrorist or adulterous politician? Who could tell them that they're wrong? *Would* they be wrong? The elected official views himself as simply fulfilling his heart's desire for a younger woman; the terrorist sees himself as doing work, work for which he will be eternally blessed. But their standards *are* subject to a higher standard; and they must not misinterpret that standard to benefit themselves.

We must adjust ourselves to God's standard, not that standard to us. And deep down, we know that because God has created us to know it. That's why we hide our wrongs. If we believed, "Well, that's just society's view," we wouldn't *sneak* into hotel rooms out of town. We know his standard—we *feel* it—because God put it inside us while we were still in our mothers' wombs. He is the architect who determines the specs. And the fact that we are all innately aware of those specs is no accident.

He offers hope that has been tested.

This world tempts us to give up. Sometimes you want to give up. No matter how deep your faith, life can throw some hard pitches at you that you aren't prepared for. And life gives you no sneak peeks at what's to come; it offers no "coming attractions" to prepare you for those unexpected pitches.

People can be cruel, and things change quickly. Everything you count on today can be gone tomorrow. Often you live feeling either pissed off or pissed on. So we *need* hope. Not hope in just anything, but hope in something tried, proven, and true. Religions come a dime a dozen. Some people worship heads of lettuce—until they get hungry. Some people worship money, until it loses its value. Others worship themselves. And we all know where that leaves us—full of ourselves and full of *it*. So when you face a mountain of despair, and the pressure of life saps every bit of your strength, you don't need a god who's hot with Madonna this month; you don't need the god whom the rapper thanks when he wins an award for his explicit material. You need the God who isn't impressed by the material girl, the God who won't be at the club popping bottles and watching his daughter on a pole. Your hope needs to be in the God who has proven himself worthy. The God with a record.

You see, hope left to itself is just an emotion. And that emotion will connect to anything that pretends to be worthy of it. If a figure named Santa Claus presents himself as one worthy of hope, then people—especially children—will put their hope in him. But since Santa isn't real (*Sorry, Zi!*), hope invested in him is hope wasted. So I don't just need someone to place my hope in, I need someone worthy of that hope. Someone for whom the evidence has come in, evidence I can sink my teeth into.

Let me just break you off a piece of the stuff I've been chewing on, stuff I hope you can sink your teeth into. One of the most remarkable things about Christianity is that it ever even got started! The earliest Christians were a bunch of guys with no style, no power, no influence. The word for them was "swagless." They were like jokes to the rest of the community; and after Christ died, these jokes were always running for their lives. And if they didn't run fast enough, and many didn't, they faced being stoned or beheaded or thrown into prison.

So nobody with any sense *wanted* to be a Christian. If you wanted to get the ladies and have everybody show you love, this Christianity boat was not what you were jumping on. For centuries it was like this. But even when it seemed that the faith was fading out or being contaminated by wicked men posing as Christians, the movement kept growing and growing. And the sojourners kept dying and dying.

Until this very day, it remains the best-known story of all time—how this big, powerful God loved His creation so much that He'd rather die for it than live without it. There are more manuscripts written about it than any other story of antiquity, more historical and archaeological evidence to show its authenticity than any other ancient event. And millions and millions of people have gone through the same storms and struggles in life that you now face and testify that the historical Christ—the Jesus of the Bible—is the very same one who answers their prayers, who comes through just when the lights are about to be cut off, who makes a way when the company is closing. He is the same God that Gertrude used to sing about when she sang, "Ain't no secret what God can do / What He's done for others / He'll do for you."

So pull out your tools of hope and faith, so you can start building today. But please follow the blueprint. Many lives have been built according to it, and you won't find a better plan on which to base your life.

Chapter Four

WHAT IS YOUR LIFE'S PURPOSE?

I'm sure you've read plenty of books. You've been to enough seminars. You've climbed every step to success. And still you feel like you're just on the second floor. Our doctors keeping writing more prescriptions for our depression, our courtrooms are filled with families fighting over kids and homes. Celebrities entertain us at the expense of their own sanity. Plastic surgery has created millions of plastic people. And still we yell, we scream, we fight, and we cry. Because, despite the bigger home, the new church location, the higher income bracket, the younger wife with a bigger ring, you still don't know . . . *you*.

It's okay. For a long time, I didn't know me, either. I don't just mean when I was growing up and struggling to find my way. I mean after I realized music was my calling, after I became successful. I had Grammys in the closet, platinum plaques on the wall, nice house, yada yada yada—but I still didn't know me.

As kids, we were told what to expect in life. Maybe you were told to get an education, to go to college if you want to be something in society, to be successful. Or maybe, like me, you were told, "You ain't nothing, your family ain't nothing; you're too slow, too dumb, and too bad to ever get out of these streets. So don't waste your time tryin'." Maybe you were told to find your niche, to reach for the stars. Perhaps you were praised all your life; perhaps you were rejected. If you were the kid always being put on a pedestal, constantly being told you were handsome or pretty, you probably became self-oriented. If you were told that you weren't as smart as your siblings or as cute as other kids, you began the uphill journey of finding a voice—struggling with pessimism, doubting every decision, never answering questions aloud in class, afraid to speak for fear of being laughed at.

Whatever you were told as a child, you started your journey to fulfill what was spoken to you. You set your "before I turn thirty" goal. Then you set your "by the time I'm fifty" goal. So now life is nothing but marks to hit instead of something to be lived.

"What do you want to be when you grow up?" we ask the little boy. "Marry a great man and have kids and you'll be happy forever," we tell the little girl.

So shortly after arriving on Planet Earth, we begin preparing for the hamster's wheel. Life becomes the pursuit of happiness and happenings marked by accomplishments and awards. From your first child's baptism to your mother's funeral. Then you retire with your little pension and 401(k) in place, grow older, and rest your head, only to return to the ground. Just part of the circle of life. But life was never meant to be a wheel. And you, my friend, are not a hamster.

And it was never meant to center on you. When we focus first and most on ourselves, it should be no surprise that our country—the richest and most influential one on the planet—is plagued by vanity, pride, ego, and arrogance. A preacher who says, "God wants you to have it all" is a danger to all who hears him. He ignores the full message of Scripture and misleads the sheep.

Something happened to me in 2002 that made me realize I

had managed to get to a different place, to step off that hamster's wheel by focusing on the important things. I had released an album that year called *The Rebirth of Kirk Franklin* that had received such great reviews and accolades in the gospel community that everybody was calling it *the* classic album of Kirk Franklin's career. But when the Grammy Award nominations came out, my name wasn't on the list. *The Rebirth* had not been nominated. Everybody around me was extremely upset, including my record company. I had a phone call with the record company executives, who are Christians. I said to them, "It's cool that I wasn't nominated. That's not why we do what we do."

I realized I had become hungry for real things, meaningful things, not these tangible, material things. The album had gone platinum and was considered a classic, but here was a lesson on how you never should put too much value in the things the world puts value in. You can pay honor to them, but never let them make you become a slave to them. Sure, I would have liked to have been recognized in that way, but I wasn't going to let that one experience own me. By my reaction, I realized something in me was changing.

These days everybody wants to get paid; everybody wants to be the star. And no one wants to be in the supporting cast. Not surprisingly, that kind of self-absorbed "me" leads to a society in which major corporate CEOs spend millions to redecorate their offices while at the same time they are laying off hundreds of employees. When you make "you" the center of life, your motives *will* be selfish. And others will be affected, kicked to the curb as you strive to either fulfill or overcome the words spoken during your youth. But at the end of the game—even with all the accomplishments and material gains—the question still remains: What have you really gained? And what did you lose to gain it? As a wise man once asked, *What does it profit us to gain the whole world if we lose our souls?* (Mark 8:36).

In that spirit, I offer a few bits of advice to save us from the hamster's wheel and keep our souls firmly in our grasp.

First, don't believe the hype.

If you never had "life" spoken into you—by that, I mean if you were given no words of encouragement and hope to start you on your way and all you ever heard were painful remarks about your body, your looks, your mind—you need to forgive those stupid people who didn't realize they were talking to greatness in the making. You were created with a divine plan already laid out for your life—even if you were born out of rape, incest, or a drunken one-night stand. "How," you might ask, "could a kind, loving God allow me to be born out of such chaos?" My answer is God does His best work when dealing with "off" circumstances— that is, with circumstances that write us off, turn us off, or piss us off. Yes, out of severe pain and confusion have come some of the most incredible lives—lives that have shaped the world.

Babe Ruth eventually became one of the greatest baseball players of all time, but Ruth was sent to an orphanage by his father when he was just seven and only one of his seven siblings survived infancy. Yet it was at the orphanage that a priest taught Ruth how to play baseball.

Legendary photographer and filmmaker Gordon Parks was not breathing when he emerged from his mother's womb, but the doctor—named Gordon—managed to revive him. The youngest of fifteen children, Gordon conquered homelessness and poverty and taught himself how to take pictures.

KFC founder Colonel Sanders often slept in the backseat of his car (sometimes with his wife, Claudia) as he traveled the country trying to convince restaurants to use his special fried chicken recipe for a franchise licensing fee. He reportedly heard the word "no" more than a thousand times on his way to becoming a business legend (all my wing and thigh people, stand up!).

But some of you may have never seen real hardship. If you have always excelled, always received the attention, always been at the top of your game whatever you do, I am blessed to give you this special word: *You ain't all that.* Please believe me, if you die, the world will not end, and *Seinfeld* will not go out of syndication. The world doesn't begin with you, and it doesn't end with you.

You may be "good people." There are many successful, attractive people in society who should feel no guilt at being blessed beyond measure. But my point simply is this: The more you have, the easier it is to think that you are above replacing. Now, God loves you, but He doesn't need you. None of us are guaranteed a spot. And you should never believe your own press. In fact, it's better not to even read it. Because you may be tempted to believe it. You may think your own hard work got you where you are. But there are geniuses with PhDs sleeping under bridges. So let us not think we have gotten here on our own. There are always others more qualified than you. But God had, *and has*, a plan for you.

Just a few more reminders.

What you do is not who you are.
One of the greatest lessons I ever learned came from a book Tony Evans gave me, called *Grace Walk* by Steve McVey. In it, he said something simple yet life-changing. He said that "what you do is not who you are." Simple, isn't it? But it hit me hard (about as hard as Gertrude did one Sunday when she caught me looking at Sister Johnson's booty while she was shouting!). He said that if he asked you who Michael Jordan is, you would answer that MJ is a basketball player. But that's not right. That's

what he does, but it isn't who he is. Who is Aretha Franklin? "She's Kirk Franklin's cousin?" *(Just playing!)* "She's a singer?" No—singing is what she does, but it isn't who she is. McVey's point is simple—what we do is *not* who we are. We are not human doings; we are human beings. And that is so important to remember, because the world you live in every day pushes you to be the hottest, the baller, the shot caller, the star.

But if you think I'm going to call you to self-humiliation, to stop striving to do your very best at whatever you are called to do, you are mistaken. This is about identity. Whatever your calling, you should pursue it as well as you possibly can; you should always strive for excellence. But it is never to be your identity.

When it comes to who you are—well, you need to think *very* carefully. When you identify yourself by your accomplishments and achievements, you set yourself up to have a name based on your performance. And when your performance changes, so does your identity. So do your best, but don't let your best be who you are. Then, whether you succeed or fail, who you truly are will never change.

When I first read that chapter in *Grace Walk,* more than ten years ago, I was at one of the lowest points of my career and ministry. I'd released a few albums that didn't sell well, I was in the middle of some legal issues with former colleagues, and I thought my relevancy was over. In the midst of that darkness, I realized that I was in the middle of a divine time-out. Since I would never have stopped the roller coaster myself, God ordained those difficult circumstances to push me to my knees, to encourage me to attend church more (because I had more time to do so!), to sit at the feet of men strong in the faith and to drink from the waters of their lives. And the lessons I learned were created for the pages of this book.

When that dark season came over my career, I was home a lot more. I had started to get used to being on the road, flying on the Concorde, always being in first class, traveling Big Willie–style. But this one night I went out to dinner in Fort Worth with my wife. We were in the middle of the meal and it occurred to both of us that we didn't really know each other that well. We almost said it at the same time: "You know what? I don't know you." I was thirty years old and we were walking into one of the darkest periods in our marriage. The problems weren't revealed until I was forced to slow down. If my career had stayed on the fast track, the big baller, we wouldn't have noticed the cracks. We hadn't realized the marriage had cracks because until then, it had been covered with trinkets, flying in and out, loving on each other for short periods, and living on the road. When we had to live with each other every day, it was like, "Wait a minute. We got married so quick that we never got to know each other." It was a four-year process that was very difficult. We came out the other end stronger in our marriage, and we love each other now more than ever. But God allowed me a divine time-out in my career so that I could focus on my marriage.

If you're at that place in your life right now, embrace those divine time-outs! It's a time to slow down, take stock, and perhaps reevaluate. I like how my man David said it in the 23rd Psalm: *He maketh me lie down.* Because we don't seem capable of making ourselves take a break when we need it.

You are becoming a person of character.

Without those divine time-outs in life handed to us by God, we would miss important opportunities to develop character. Those opportunities are all around us—the family member who drives you crazy also gives you the opportunity to put that Sunday sermon on patience into practice; the coworker in a bad marriage who gets talked about at the water cooler gives you the opportunity to practice a self-control that helps you to avoid the trap of being drawn into other people's problems, the opportunity to stop thinking just about yourself and your world.

Character. That thing that makes your eyes glow and causes people to wonder why little things don't drive you crazy. It is the missing piece to the common good, deeply needed inside each of us. It isn't something that will naturally develop. It must be pursued, chased after, factored into the equation of who you are and who you're going to be. And every opportunity to develop character must be seized. If not, you become a grown-up who still acts like a child. You become a person with no ethics or morals when it comes to your business transactions. You don't learn how to fight fair. You never become a leader who changes things—at least, not for the good. You become like your old high school friends who only want to talk about "what we did in high school," about "back in the day." Because that was the last time their lives were worth talking about.

The reason politicians lie to us term after term is that they don't have character. The reason we have drama in our homes is that we aren't a people of character. There are many complex reasons for wars and global conflicts, but if the individuals involved had genuine character and true integrity, peace talks would end up being more than just a sizzle reel for CNN. We would see people—we would see ourselves—serving and sacrificing for the good of others; and it wouldn't be just for appearances, but for real change. That's why every difficult situation, every storm in life that comes your way, has to be viewed with an eye on the truth that God allows hard times in our lives to build and develop our character; therefore, you can't run away from every trial that comes. Because if you do, you won't grow.

I have a friend who is divorced and her son is hurting because every time he spends time with his dad, all they do are things his dad likes to do. The dad played sports for a living, and when they are together they either play basketball or play video games about basketball. That is his idea of "quality time." But the boy wants more. He wants to talk, to learn, to grow from his father. But because his dad never learned the game of life off the court, he doesn't know those "plays." And because he chooses not to hear his son, and just blows off his feelings as immature or "that's your mama talking," he's missing a divine moment to grow himself, to learn how to enjoy something that's outside of his normal world. See, the father's game may be over, but his son's game has just begun. Now it's time to sacrifice what's comfortable for what's important. This way, two people can develop character at the same time.

Never forget: How you see the problem *is* the problem. From time to time, my trainer at the gym will increase my weights. Sometimes he'll put weights on that I think are impossible for me to lift. I'll remind him that I'm a little dude and can't lift as much as the big boys. He doesn't pay me any attention; he just says, "I'm your trainer; I know how much you can lift because I've been training you for years. And even if it's too heavy, I'm behind you for the purpose of spotting you; so just in case you can't, I'm here to help you get the weight up." If I sit there and argue with him about the weight, I miss an opportunity to get bigger and stronger; plus, I waste time.

So it's in my best interest to "trust my trainer" and lift what He has put on the bench (if I were Baptist, I would start whooping about now). Not to lift what He has put on my bench is to miss a chance to grow. If you want character, you've gotta lift the weights. They're all around you, on your job, in your home, in your marriage. You can be lazy all you want; you can say, "That ain't got nuthin' to do with me. That ain't my business." But if we are a great chain linked together as people created in the image of God, what happens to you *does* affect me. The fifteen-year-old girl who was gang-raped in Richmond, California, after her homecoming dance was watched by onlookers for more than two hours before some girls heard it was going on and called the police. Nobody saw it as their business, so she suffered for hours being raped again and again because none of those little punks would speak up. See how dangerous it is to have those weights sitting around and never see the need to lift them up? To tackle the heavy things, the difficult things, so that when trouble or difficulties come, you've done the work, you've built the muscles. You're not scared anymore to say to the crowd around you, "This ain't right!" It's time to say something; it's time for change! Lift those weights.

Stay focused on your education.

When I was growing up, there wasn't a lot of emphasis put on education. My aunt Gertrude had a fourth-grade education and she didn't stress education with me; in the community I lived in, school wasn't something people emphasized or asked you about. You didn't walk to the corner and have people ask you how you were doing in school. That didn't really happen until I turned thirteen—and then it was somebody saying, "You need to stop messing up in school." But they wouldn't sit me down and have an encouraging conversation with me about how important education is. What happens is when a person has other strengths that excite people, they put the emphasis on those. If you're a sports or music prodigy in the hood, that's what gets all the attention.

When I think back on my time in high school, it was amazing the things I was allowed to get away with. At O. D. Wyatt High School in Fort Worth, all the artsy classes were down this one hall that was kind of out of the way. The choir room, the band room, the drama room, all were in a row down that hall. And my homeroom teacher coincidentally was the drama teacher, so I started the day (and the drama) on that hall. I got so excited about all that energy in the hall that those were the only classes I went to. And nobody ever checked me on it! I never went to biology or math; I just stayed in that hall, cutting all those classes I had no interest in attending. There was only one time I can remember somebody saying something to me about it. I was fifteen and there was this guy who was a junior. He went to the church I was playing music for at the time. He was popular at Wyatt and spent time every day working in the office. One day I got in trouble and wound up at the office. He pulled me into a room, closed the door, and wore me out. "Nigga [that's what he said], you trippin'! You up here acting a fool! If you think I'm gonna let you off just cause you my boy, you got it twisted!" That made quite an impact on me. But it wasn't enough. I dropped out at seventeen.

So now here I am twenty years later, and everywhere I turn I see the consequences of my failure to get an adequate education. There have been times when I didn't fully understand a contract, or didn't fully understand a royalty rate, or didn't have the education to dive deep into the business. I have seen how my career has suffered because of it. There are so many things that could have been better for my family if I had an education. What happens all too common is that you overlook what you're missing and learn to make do without it. You coast along and do such a good job at coasting that you probably even forget about it and the people around you forget about it, too, because it's not really affecting them, so what do they care? Then you start having children and you see them struggling in school and you aren't able to help them. My wife got pregnant in college and never finished, but she's a very smart woman. She is able to handle their work. But now, especially with the two young ones, we put such an emphasis on education. Not just education in school but education in life. For example, my son, who is nine, is very talented on the drums. They've been having him play at the church for the kids' choir, which sings every fifth Sunday. One Sunday, my son was just all over the place when he was playing. Musicians have this saying called "playing in the pocket." That means you're playing with everybody else, playing within the band. It's clear that it ain't about you. When I saw Caziah playing for himself rather than with the band, I was thinking, *Who does he think he is?* Tammy was telling me that it wasn't that bad. But I said, "Yes, it is." I don't want my son doing all that stuff and when he gets older he can't get a gig because nobody wants to play with him. But when I was talking with him about it later, he said the ladies over at the choir are telling him to play like that. I said, "You tell them your father said he wants you to learn how to play in a band. It's not the Caziah show. Tell them your daddy wants you to learn it the right way." But there it was—some ladies were about to let him get away with something that's not good for a musician, because of his skill. But because of what I've learned in life, I'm not going to let him get away with it. We're making him take classes, so he can study the gift. He'll be able to get more gigs if he plays with more discipline and can sight read.

The words "discipline" and "education" go hand in hand. You have to have discipline to go to class, to sit and listen to lectures, to go home and do your homework. The people who go to class and sit there and then go home and do the work—I'm amazed by that. But nothing about that in our society is painted as sexy.

So we're back to the non-sexies. This society is going to hell in a handbasket if we do not prioritize the non-sexies. Again, that list of non-sexies, that's the stuff that creates the discipline, the character, the essence, the substance, the maturity, that balance. It's not the stuff that gets you on the cover of magazines. You know what I think we ought to do? We need to go to those people, those celebrities that influence the culture, and we need to ask them, "Why are you just promoting the hot new liquor, or the next sneaker?" We need celebrities to turn their voices up more about how important it is to have an education. It's never too late to go back to get an education for yourself, to educate yourself in nontraditional ways (for example, by using the public library as your own personal resource, taking a class in something you're interested in, or asking someone whose work you admire to teach you what they know), and it's equally important to encourage your kids to try their hardest at school, and make them understand how important education is. It's the only way we're going to get kids to listen. And while we're at it, we have to get these teachers more money. We've got to make teachers feel like the world is depending on them, that the value of our society is on their shoulders. Teachers must be looked at as a third spouse—no one can have your child that long every day and not be influencing that child. You've got to have them on your team. We have to take the mind-set of a professional sports team—when they have a star, they try to find ways to use that player within the system, and also to keep that player safe because they know the championship will be won on that player's shoulders. Well, if your child is going to be a champion, it's going to be resting a lot on the teachers' shoulders. We've got to find a way to big them up. Perhaps we can do to them what we do to military personnel when we see them walking down the street or at the airport. People stop and shake their hands and thank them. We need to do that for teachers, too. Teachers, make some noise!

Run from the VIP section.
You see, the system that society puts on us makes us slaves to our accomplishments. Those who accomplish more gain more. They get more perks; they get more access. Who doesn't want to be inside the velvet rope? Who doesn't want to feel like an insider?

So you do whatever you have to do to get and keep the access. And this creates a whirlpool of nonstop performance. When my albums were flying off the shelf, I was getting calls to sit courtside with some of the most powerful. I was a gospel artist who had carte blanche to any event you could name. If my kids wanted to say "hi" to the Jonas Brothers, I'd just pass them the phone. Miley Cyrus told me she loved my music. I told her my daughter is a fan of hers. Next thing I know, Kennedy is in the front row at the concert.

I'm talking about access. Box seats at concerts. Backstage passes. The flight is full, your assistant can't get you on; you call yourself, shake a few hands, take some pictures, and you're on. Upgraded, too. Do you see how dangerous that can be? And when you taste that, you will do *anything* to keep it. Even if you *are* a gospel artist. It doesn't matter. You've become what you do. So when you stop doing what you do, you feel—the operative word is "feel"—you're no longer who you are. So you do whatever you need to do to keep the access, so you can stay who you are.

Whether it's big corporate America, sports, entertainment, or the normal everyday nine-to-five, everyone feels this pull on some level. And we end up not knowing who we are or why we're unhappy. Millions of dollars are spent trying to make people happy. Trying to give people shortcuts to happiness. But there *is* no shortcut to character and endurance. Maybe that's why we don't see more of it.

You ever wonder why animals at the zoo seem to have a little edge on them? The tiger never quite looks totally happy. The monkeys seem to have a lot on their minds. I think that's because they know that they aren't living out their full potential. I've been to Africa. Several times. I've seen lions running free in Africa. And compared to the ones in the San Diego Zoo, there is a different bounce in their step. More cockiness in their roar.

The difference? The lion in the zoo is just existing; the one in the wild is living. The animal in the jungle lives out the purpose he was created for. He reigns over his dominion.

I hope you understand the difference here. We're talking about something crucial in the building of a blueprint.

Understand the difference between having a job and having a calling.

You see, a job doesn't create in you a burning sense of purpose, a motivation for living. It doesn't fire you up in the morning as you look forward to the day; it doesn't make you believe that something special will happen today because you were created for that something. No, a job doesn't do that for your soul. A job just means a paycheck, money to pay the electric bill or get the brakes fixed. You dread going to work; while you're there, you check the clock every hour, praying for the day to just end.

But a calling speaks to that dream you had as a little kid, when you were drawing pictures or fixing things around the house with the toy tools you got for Christmas. It fulfills you like nothing else in the world. Before I started recording music, I worked several jobs just to get by. I sold shoes at Kinney Shoes (anybody remember *Kinney Shoes*?). I worked at a grocery store bagging food, mopping floors, and restocking shelves. Every break I had was spent trying to do music. If I took a bathroom break, I was writing songs on the toilet (too much information?). If there was a music event in town, I would stay up all night and then go straight to work. It didn't bother me to catch a bus, borrow money, stand outside for hours, or do whatever I had to do *because I had a dream*. No matter how many times my car got repo'd, I found a way. I felt a calling to do music. When other musicians in town wouldn't do a certain event because the money wasn't right, I did it for free. I didn't care. I had a burning passion to play, to write; and if I had to, I would have paid them. My jobs didn't give me that fire; my calling did.

But if your mind is preoccupied with just existing, you will make the dangerous choice of money over purpose. More money may be connected to the job, but fulfillment and longevity come from your calling and purpose. What's the use of having a Range Rover if you hate waking up every day to go to a job you can't stand just to pay for it? If a smaller car and less expensive house allow you to do something that creates a glow, something that lasts long past next year's new truck model—well, forget the car, forget the designer clothes, never mind the suburbs, you're living now! And the existing—well, leave that for King Kong at the zoo.

Be a missionary. Teach elementary school. Fix up that old house that's *paid for*! Stop looking at the Joneses, the Rodriguezes, the Diddys. Realize that what you have ain't bad. And just because they have more doesn't mean they *really* have more.

Why are you here?

You are God's supreme masterpiece. The God of all creation crafted you for His signature collection. You may not feel like it; you may not always act like it. Maybe you haven't accepted it. You may even be living in denial, refusing to accept it. But that doesn't change who you are. Or what you were created to be.

You were created for something big. You were created for God's glory. Now, this isn't pop theology I'm giving you. And you don't have to fall down or speak in tongues. But believe me—He takes pride in *you*. And every morning He breathes new life into your body.

If tomorrow you lose everything—you are laid off from your job, rejected by your friends, betrayed by your spouse—you will *still* be a work of art, one formed, sculpted, painted by the greatest artist the universe has ever known. Your job, your friends, your spouse, your status in society—none of these makes you, you.

You are no mistake, no accident. And no luck was involved in your creation. As a Christian, I have learned—and am *still* learning—to reject titles and labels, to just see myself as a fully loved son. Now I know that if I sucked at everything I did, it would not change the way God sees me. And that takes away the pressure to perform. If my albums go copper or aluminum, I'm still a winner in His eyes. Some people may think it corny to see things this way, but people who have lived their lives on the hamster's wheel—that never-ending show with no intermission—can feel my pain. And they know that being free to fail without losing your spot in God's heart takes a load off your life.

I used to hate Kirk; I had *always* hated him. He was (and still is!) short, ugly (not as much), not very well-liked—until he sat at a piano. Girls didn't much like me. And I didn't have many friends. So whatever I had to do to be liked, that's what I did. I was a performer. And I brought that mind-set into my adult relationships, even into my faith. I thought that if I did more, prayed more, gave more, was nicer to people, God would like me more.

Then one Sunday I heard that nothing I could ever do could make God like me more. That was foreign to me. And confusing. Everyone I knew liked me for what I did, but then I heard for the first time that God loves me for who I am. And He loves me too much to let me stay what I am.

When I first sold a million copies of a record, I thought a million people liked me. And when an album would only go gold, I thought that half those million people didn't like me anymore. What a sad way to live! These people don't know me. They don't know what I had for dinner. Or what I cried about in bed. They know my music, but they don't know me. Because, as I've learned, I am *not* what I do. Although I am incredibly blessed to have such a passion for what I do and have worked hard to reach people with my gift.

Nobody else could ever be you, and you deserve a standing ovation.

You are so special that someone saw you as worth dying for—even though He knew every mistake you would ever make and every rejection you would ever receive. And that shows you were meant to live for so much more than a hamster's wheel. Inside you is untapped greatness that no tight dress, no new nose, no faster car, no new belly ring could ever bring out. And what does it matter if the world applauds you but the one who created you never claps His hands because your life was not lived for Him?

A famous young violin player from Europe made his American debut at Madison Square Garden. There was great excitement about hearing him play in person, so tickets were sold out months in advance. The who's who of entertainment and the press were there just to be in the presence of this young phenomenon. As he took the stage, you could hear a pin drop. He began to play his first notes. The sound filled the rafters. Grown men fought desperately to hold back tears from the piercing melody of his violin. By the time he played the last line of one of the most difficult romantic pieces ever written, the crowd needed a long pause just to catch their breath. They applauded wildly, like their lives were being saved. The enthusiasm and pandemonium made the Garden seem like a madhouse. As the crowd stood applauding, the young maestro looked into the audience and then ran offstage. With the crowd looking on in confusion, his manager followed close behind. The manager, not knowing why the young musician had run away in the middle of such grand acceptance of his work, begged him to come back onstage. The violinist responded sadly, "Did you see the gentleman in the front row not standing?" The manager had no idea what he was talking about because the whole house had been standing in appreciation. And they were begging for an encore. Then the young man explained: "The man in the front row with his legs crossed, not applauding—that's my music teacher. So nothing else matters."

What does it matter if the world applauds you, tells you that you're great, gives you its approval, but the one who gave you breath, life, and purpose is not applauding? Whatever you do, if it doesn't matter to Him, then it simply doesn't matter. All that we do should be done for an audience of one.

If you don't know who you are, go back to the manufacturer.

Despite where we are as a culture and our belief that we don't need God, we must understand that everyone and everything in our lives that we use to define ourselves is limited. Let me explain. Even your parents, on their best day, can only equip you for what they *hope* you will become. After all their hard work and the life lessons they tried to instill in you, it is always possible— quite possible—that your life won't go the way they've planned. Even the most prestigious universities can't guarantee a successful career and a six-figure income, much less a happy, prosperous lifestyle. No finite thing can tell you what your tomorrow will look like. So it's in your best interest to connect with the infinite who not only sees today and why you were created for it, but who also knows what your tomorrow looks like and has plans to help you get there and beyond.

Overlooking that reality simply prevents you from truly understanding who you are, why you are here, and how you can fulfill your divine purpose.

When the plans don't seem to make sense, go back to the architect. Or else you'll waste a lot of time staring at papers you don't understand. And if you try to go it on your own, you'll build something that's not safe. So go to the one who thought up the building and has the perfect plans for you to build your life by. When your life is filled with lies, misinformation, mistrust, and rejection, go to the manual—*the* Word. How can you trust it? Visit some of His other buildings. Yes, some have faults, but many have been standing strong for as long as time itself.

If you are filled with envy or jealousy for what others have and what their lives are like, you won't celebrate your own originality. Your fingerprint is a one-of-a-kind mark on this planet. No one has the same print as you. How you walk is unique to you. No other human being is put together in quite the same intricate way as you are. To focus on being and having what belongs to others is to distract yourself; it prevents you from accomplishing what you have been created to do and become.

Can't you see how jealousy and comparing yourself to others can take you off course? There are people in this world who only you can touch. God has placed certain individuals in your life to receive what only you can give them. You may think you have nothing to offer, that there is nothing in you that someone else could need. And your self-image may be so poor that imagining yourself as valuable to others seems impossible. But the truth remains—your very existence means that you are here not just to take up oxygen; continuing to compare yourself to others robs you by keeping you from recognizing this truth: You are *great* at being you, but *horrible* at being them. Never forget that!

I am not always a fan of everything I do musically, but one song that I can say was a gift sent to me from God—first-class delivery—is a song called "Imagine Me." In that song, the lyrics speak so deeply to this subject of reminding yourself to see you the way God sees you. I happened to be walking by the mirror in the bathroom while working on the song. I had a melody but I didn't have any lyrics yet. I glanced in the mirror and out came these words: "Imagine me, loving what I see when the mirror looks at me. Imagine me, in a place of no insecurities, and I'm finally happy cause I, I imagine me." Then this beautiful chorus dropped into my head and it said, "Imagine me, being free, trusting you, totally; finally, I can imagine me. I admit it was hard to see, you being in love with someone like me. Finally, I can . . . imagine me."

I called my wife upstairs to listen to it, because I wasn't confident that a song about imagining oneself through God's eyes would connect with people. I thought maybe it was trying to be too deep. As I played the song, I saw tears start to run down the cheeks of this beautiful mother of my children. The words touched her right away. Even with her obvious outer beauty, she needed to be reminded of God's unconditional love as she "imagined me."

The reason why you see so little originality in the world—especially in music and entertainment—is because everybody wants to chase what's hot, what's popular. The world says, "Give us another one of those." And so we try to copy what's successful. Every song on the radio sounds the same, every movie has the same plot. Being original means taking a risk. And that's, well, risky. But without risks, without taking a chance, everything ends the same. So take a risk: Love what you have and love who you are.

Your life is not a destination but a journey.

Many people are bitter and frustrated because their lives are not what they were told they would be. They had a dream, a plan, but nothing about their lives has gone according to the plan. Or they are so busy trying to make that picture come true that, in everything they do, they focus so completely on reaching that goal, that dream, that picture of what happiness looks like.

Please know that happiness and joy are two different things. Happiness depends on the happenings around you, but joy is that inner peace you have regardless of whether you reach that goal. Because, you realize, you are still you without it. Nothing external makes you who you are.

You don't want happiness; you want joy. Because when nothing is happening, you're no longer happy. But when you get laid off from your job, you can still have joy. When the engagement is called off, your joy is still turned on. Friends abandon you, but your joy is still there. Your body isn't as tight as it was in high school, and your hairline keeps going back farther and farther, and that left knee—Lord, that knee! It gives you problems every time you play basketball with your son. But your joy is as fresh and new as the day you were born. Nothing on the outside can take this away from you on the inside.

If you say that's unrealistic, it's because you've never had it. I wouldn't sell it if I didn't believe in the product.

So in this pursuit of happiness *(Sorry, Will!)*, we chase whatever looks like it will make us happy. But in that pursuit, many sunsets, many baseball games, many dances, many picnics are missed or even overlooked. Because we're so busy trying to get "there." But where is "there"? What does it look like? And how do you know when you've found it? At the pace we travel to get "there," we're tired, worn out, and have no character to be able to live there responsibly even if we do find it. We might be happy, but we never develop character and don't experience joy.

Man, it's not about the destination; it's all about the journey.

I live in Texas. And when I started traveling, one of our first big trips was to Los Angeles. We loaded up the tour bus, but we left so late we had to race the whole way to get to the concert on time. When we got there, people asked me how I liked the road trip. They asked me about the sunset in the mountains, the stars that shined on us through the desert, and the bright lights of Vegas. Man, I didn't see *any* of that. We were so busy hurrying to get there, I missed the beauty of the trip. In other words, we were so busy trying to get to our "there" that we missed all the beauty of the journey.

The storms you face in your life—the trials and the tears of your first heartbreak, that difficult pregnancy (which, by God's grace, ended with the doctor handing you a new gift), the hard choices that you had to make about your aging mother moving in—those are the sunsets and mountains on your journey. Those are the things that produce the character you need, the joy you've been looking for. They make your life spicy, intriguing, melodic—so that others want to sing it. It is your commitment to life's journey that makes it beautiful and sweet. Take the five-step plan off the fridge, turn off the self-help channels, stop living for someday—"*someday* I'm gonna do this, *someday* I'm gonna do that; and *then* I'll be happy"—and just live. Make mistakes. Fall but get back up. Learn the first time, so the lesson won't have to be repeated. Love God; serve others. And remember: God has not given us a spirit of fear but of power, love, and a sound mind.

Can you imagine looking in the mirror and loving what you see? Big belly; freckled nose; thick lips; one big toe longer than the other; in a wheelchair but the wheelchair is not you; short; tall; black, brown, beige, or purple; slanted-eyed or cross-eyed—we look just like our Father. Every one of us. Can you imagine that? Pursue your dreams, but don't lose yourself during the chase. Imagine you!

Chapter Five

LIFESCAPING

Many people enjoy gardening, but few enjoy dealing with weeds. For most gardeners, weeds pose a frustrating and ever-present problem. But if you want a lush garden, one filled with pretty flowers or delicious, bodacious vegetables, you *must* deal with weeds. Otherwise, the ugliness of the weeds will over-shadow the beauty of everything else. And neighborhood discussions will settle on your garden for the wrong reasons. We have talked a lot about creating a strong and sturdy foundation, but there's no denying the fact that people won't even be able to see the sturdiness of the foundation if they are distracted by all the unattractive, unsightly things you have allowed to spread around in your life. All the effort you've put into your blueprint will be for nothing if your life is still cluttered with ugly weeds that can overrun even the healthiest foundation. I guarantee you that the lazy gardener—the one who puts no time into weed maintenance—will never receive "garden of the month" honors, nor will she be able to truly enjoy the beauty of that which she has created.

Would-be gardeners who simply talk about having beautiful, productive gardens but spend their weekends in front of the TV playing Guitar Hero, spending only enough time outdoors to drop some fertilizer here and there—well, they are really wasting their time. The lady who complains to anyone and everyone about her frustration with the "weed issue," the city's irrigation problems, or global warming's negative effect on her soil may win some "amens" from her bored audience. But she will have neither awards nor pictures of flourishing flowers and vegetables to be proud of. She certainly won't reap the produce earned by the hands of the other committed, sacrificial, uncomplaining gardeners.

As the garden goes, so goes life. The careers, families, homes, and spiritual lives we yearn for don't just appear because we desire them. They don't happen simply because we wish for them, pray for them, or even fast for them. They come only to those who, when the prayer meeting has ended and the church doors are locked, water the seeds that have been planted from Scripture, fertilize the thoughts and experiences provided by God's spirit. And who have a zero-tolerance policy when it comes to weeds. If you want a healthy life, you *must* deal with the weeds of negative thoughts, hangers-on relationships, and, of course, the player haters—you've heard the term before, those critical people who want to trash all your desires and dreams. But if you deal diligently with those weeds, working daily to remove their influences from your life, you will enjoy good fruit—a healthy attitude, stable home, strong marriage, and inner peace, even in the midst of great stress.

What you sow . . . well, you know the rest.
I have weeds that I need to deal with, and you do, too. And until we realize that truth, we will talk about weeds, perhaps even cut

the tops off weeds during the halftimes of our lives, but their ugliness will continue to crowd out everything else in our gardens. We can dress up ourselves and our families and parade in front of our friends, in front of church groups, in front of people we think should feel blessed to be in our presence. We might manage to make our exteriors *look* impressive, but the weeds beneath the surface—the weeds within all of us—will keep us from truly flourishing. And smiling.

Without attention to the weeds, all our other activities—having children, saying "I do," earning that promotion at work—are just time-outs in a game that someday will end. The biggest problems in our homes, lives, relationships, involve weeds we let grow unchecked because dealing with them requires honesty. *Yes, we've got to be honest.* And that, my friend, looking deep into the mirror of your soul, is the hardest job ever.

As much as I love being a father, I am not by nature a fan of traditional parenting. By traditional, I mean parenting engaged in the details of your child's life—the kind of parenting that makes time around the dinner table for questions about the day, that finds a teachable moment while explaining to a twelve-year-old why the Jonas Brothers can't just show up at her birthday party. By nature, I am selfish. *Very* selfish. I like my "me" time. Getting deep into my children's lives does not come easily for me. I never saw it modeled, so it was a behavior I had to learn later in life.

As much as I love my wife, I am not by nature inclined to listen to all her stories or watch her favorite soaps with her. And my flesh would love the opportunity to step out every now and then and kick it with the fellas and do what feels good to it, because it's the flesh.

As much as I want to give in church, at times I can't help thinking it would be great to keep my 10 percent and get more stuff that I want. *I told you I'm selfish; it's my nature.*

As much as I love church and being around brothers and sisters in the faith, some of us can be corny. *Very* corny. When some people become "born-again," they seem to lose their style, all their swag, their understanding of what's happening in the world. They have no idea what MySpace or Facebook is (or, at least, so they say), they don't know that Donnie Simpson is no longer on BET, that men with cornrows or earrings aren't necessarily going to hell, that wearing no makeup doesn't mean looking more spiritual (makeup can at times be a blessing of disguise!).

As much as I love Barack Obama—forgive me, *President* Barack Obama!—I hate that not agreeing with all his policies and views seems to some people less black or less supportive of the brother. The election of the first African-American president is historic, but the president's skin color doesn't give him a pass when it comes to being held accountable; and it doesn't obligate me to agree with everything he does or says. I can still celebrate our progress while not always agreeing with the plan. I guarantee you that the First Lady doesn't always agree with him about which movie to see on their next date night or which university the girls should attend when they grow up. But at the end of the day, that's her baby—Barack Hussein Obama.

I love my beautiful dark brown, chocolate, paper sack brown, high yellow brothers and sisters. But our color doesn't give us a pass either. History may have given us a limp, but we must refuse to allow it to keep us from running. "The Man" isn't making us talk loud in restaurants, name our kids after alcohol (little Alizé), or wear rollers in our hair and house shoes to the mall wearing "Barack is my homeboy" T-shirts.

Now, I've traveled all over the world and have seen no place like America. And I love this country's diversity. Still, I need my white brothers and sisters not to blow off what they hear from the hearts of black people as simply unjustified anger, anguish, and pain. I agree that black leaders sometimes curse the darkness without celebrating the light. But even as our Jewish brothers and sisters continue to struggle with the aftermath of the Holocaust, we face the struggle of learning what freedom looks like all these years after the Emancipation Proclamation was signed. Ol' Abe, if his motives were pure, should have followed it up with a "now what." But he didn't, so many of us are learning as we go.

We love the idea of God—or some spiritual being—watching over us, but *not* of him telling us what to do. We love taking Christmas pictures with the family, but *not* dealing with the fact that someone in the shot has a drug problem. Or that someone else in it needs a place to crash for a few weeks because she is tired of being beaten by a husband who sits on the deacon board at church but won't make time to lead the home. We love scientific theories because they fool us into thinking we don't need God. After all, if we can explain the world without Him, maybe we can even live without Him, because we're selfish. Remember? But we still want beautiful, productive gardens.

So as I write for people who have read "how to" and "how come" books, I realize that everyone is jaded. Including me. Cable news has jaded me. Relationships have jaded me. Movies that show people being blown up, along with pretty girls who never have stretch marks, have jaded me. Big ministries have jaded me. Small churches in drug-ridden communities have jaded me. *MTV Cribs* has jaded me. Celebrity marriages that last as long as a good haircut have jaded me. I've been desensitized and at times have a very pessimistic attitude.

Still, I write another book—a book about faith, a book about family, a book about the savior of the world. And while I write it, I try to keep my relevancy and my swagger. Because even though I sometimes sound angry and frustrated at all the institutions I'm supposed to believe in—institutions that are, in many respects, broken—still I believe.

I believe the journey to healing begins when we admit our sickness. No doctor prescribes medication without first asking, "Where does it hurt?" I am reminded of people who have died from diseases that could have been treated if caught in their early stages but who wouldn't seek help when symptoms first appeared. Refusing to hear bad news doesn't take the bad away.

Before we go any further, I must explain something. I am, by nature, a doubter. I hesitate to believe in anything. I think that's important to explain, because most would assume that my faith shapes my outlook. And you might expect that, being written by someone who is unapologetically Christian, this book will have an always sunny, upbeat outlook. That expectation might be reasonable, but it's not true.

From day one, believing in God has been work for me. Trusting what I can't see has *always* been a work in progress. So when I encourage you to believe with me that a divine plan is being worked out in each individual's life, that mere chance (such as an animals-to-men happenstance) must always be viewed as a mere theory, I'm speaking not as a super-religious Sunday school teacher, but as one who has found hope in the midst of chaos. And believe me, I looked for every reason *not* to believe.

When I look honestly at my church, there are things that disturb me. One of the big ones is the mask. In many cases, as soon as you walk through the church door, you get handed the mask. You don't even realize they're handing it to you; sometimes you even hand it to yourself. *Welcome, come on in. Please put this mask on.* What happens in church is what I call the "hospital effect." When you're struggling, instead of people saying, "You struggling with that? Me, too," what you get is a lot of people trying to fix you. But many of the people trying to fix you are sick themselves. It's a lot easier to fix you and inspire you and motivate you and remind you than to try to do those things to myself. That takes a lot more work. Like I've stated before, with

Gertrude everything I did was wrong, whether it was in the church or out of the church. I think I became numb to that. I loved to dance, and there was this skating rink called Jolly Time that would turn into something like a teen club at some point in the night. They would still be skating around, but in the middle we'd be dancing. It was the spot! So one time this gospel group that I was singing with heard I was up at the rink, and they came there, got on the mic, and blasted me in front of the whole skating rink, talking about how was I supposed to be singing to the Lord when I was up there skating and dancing. That's the type of world I grew up in, with all this condemnation. So having faith and trusting in God and believing has been very difficult because you are used to *so* much bad. Even when things are good, you are still looking over your shoulder just waiting for the bad to come back. Someone once said something to me that cut pretty deep: *It's hard to see God's love as a father when you've never had one.* It's hard for some black men to develop a relationship with Christ when all they're presented with is a picture of someone who looks to them like oppression—a white man with blue eyes. I can definitely identify with these struggles, but I managed to work through them and *still* believe.

If you don't know me, you might be asking, "What makes Kirk qualified to speak on these issues? What school did he attend? What is his background? What makes his view correct on issues that have polarized societies from the beginning of creation? Isn't he some non–Ivy League, non–seminary trained, non-evangelical, non-liberal black man from the South? What qualifies *him* to speak to these matters? How dare he?"

Well, let me establish my credentials, my bona fides, when it comes to discussing the weeds that can litter a garden.

As I told you before, when I was four years old, I was adopted by a sixty-four-year-old woman named Gertrude. My biological mother played the role of a distant big sister who came around from time to time to drop off Christmas gifts and show off her newest boyfriend. My biological father provided me a haircut when I was six. That was the first and last thing the man would ever do for me. Years later, when I was grown, he did show up backstage at one of my concerts asking for VIP passes. *(Thanks, Dad!)* I have a younger sister whose life has mostly been spent on drugs, selling her body, and in prison. Weeds in abundance.

I was raised in the African-American church community where much of the culture was based not on what you know but on how you feel. Sex was a big part of our upbringing; from the church to the streets and back again. What we did in one affected what we did in the other. In the summers, we had no adult supervision; the lack of affirmation and love at home caused us to look for them in one another at very young ages. At six and seven years old, we were introduced to things that children should be protected from. And a lot of that introduction came from people we saw as protectors. There were a lot of men in the black church gospel community who would try to do things to the young boys in the church. They would approach some of the young boys, maybe touch a leg or try to hit on you, and as a little boy that's very scary. These grown men should have been our protectors, but instead of protecting us some of these older dudes were turning some of these boys out and having relationships with them. It's similar to what's been happening in the Catholic church. Even some of the older women would be doing it, too, trying to holler at the young boys and even sometimes giving them some. So you're a young boy, eleven, twelve, thirteen years old, and you have this older lady trying to do whatever she wanted to you. You were not protected. One time when I was about nine or ten, I was playing for a youth musical at a church in Fort Worth. There was a very popular musician in town and, because I was kind of like his protégé, this guy would come pick me up for the practices. One evening when he was bringing me home, he tried to approach me and he said something nasty to me. There were many things Gertrude did wrong, but one thing she did do to protect me was she would go to the men at the church that she considered straight and she would tell them, *Watch after my boy.* Sometimes men would come up to her and point out different guys and tell her, *He needs to stay away from that one because he'll try to turn him out.*

This may sound outrageous, and you may be tempted to condemn the entire black church after reading it, but I would ask you to give it some perspective. There are crooked police, but no one suggests that we do away with the criminal justice system. There are crooked politicians, but we aren't trying to scrap the whole political system. The church seems to be the only institution in our society that everyone wants to shut down when we hear about some crookedness. I have sat at the table with the presidents of countries in Africa and I have even heard an African president say, *We need to apologize to our African-American brothers for selling them into slavery.* But we don't stick our middle finger up to Africa and say, "We ain't never coming back here!"

I got into a lot of trouble as a kid. From fights to defend myself as a church kid being raised by an older lady to fights to defend my masculinity from people who drew conclusions from my size and involvement in choirs filled with effeminate men. So trying both to prove myself and to heal wounds from the lack of mama's love, I became promiscuous with many young women.

I messed up a lot in school. Drinking, drugs, trying to be that dude on the block—I broke my mother's heart. I failed my freshman year in high school. And I even paid for an abortion when I was a teenager. By the age of seventeen, I had dropped out of high school; I also had a child on the way. Then, a couple of years later, the lady who took in a snotty-nosed kid and gave him her name was found in bed late one night; as I banged on the door, the last breath had already left Gertrude's body. These were all weeds with which I've had to grapple.

Dreaming was a luxury I couldn't afford. Managing a garden was out of the question. Little did I know that every experience, every failure, every night I spent hating life, every death of a childhood friend, every sermon, every word from Gertrude, was a seed that would sprout into something that neither I nor religion nor science could ever take credit for.

Luck rolls dice; chance wins bingo. But a rose growing through the cement is a phenomenon that only the heavens can explain or take credit for. The sovereign hand of the divine gardener knows how much fertilizer to use in this area, how much water to use in that one. How? For one thing, he's been working in gardens for a long time; and for another, he's also the one who establishes the limits of the gardens and the rules that make them grow.

I've had dinner in the White House; I've waited in holding cells to see cracked-out loved ones. I've had photo ops with presidents, pimps, ball players, and pastors. I've stood on stage next to Billy Graham and R. Kelly. I've cried at the funerals of gay men; I've fought with guys who think that sleeping around with many women is just what we do. I stay frustrated with the evangelical right and am constantly afraid of the left. My best friends include people with PhDs and those with criminal records, people who own cars and those who make cars, and some who have recently had cars repo'd. I'm open, but I believe in absolutes; I'm not as selfish as I used to be, and I'm still learning how to manage my garden. Let me share with you some of the things I have learned as I have put lifescaping to work in Kirk Franklin's world.

Don't become addicted to other people's drama.

If you find yourself sucked into your girlfriend's problems with her man or your homeboy's problems with all of his stuff like you are watching some good reality TV, that is an unhealthy relationship. At least on reality television you always have the opportunity to change the channel. Other people's drama can be very addictive. But at least on TV there is a barrier; in real life we get sucked in and there's no barrier to protect us. What you must understand is that relationships have a spiritual essence to them. After a while you begin to partake in their mind-set, their way of looking at life. They don't like men, so you don't like men. They say the sky is gray, so you see everything as gray. Some people see a conspiracy theory in everything; so now you start seeing a conspiracy around every corner.

God gave us the power of choice for a reason. Use it.

A while back I made the decision to not hang around married men who did not like marriage. This is a choice I made for the sake of my own marriage. I knew those kind of men and their mind-set would only hurt my bond with my wife. No matter how interesting the person or friend, I continue to stick by the decision, even if it means I have to spend some time by myself. As a married dude, I don't have a lot of homeboys to kick it with as a result of this choice. So my circle of friends is very small. But what's so fresh about God is that he presents everything in life as a choice. In the Bible, you see God talking to Israel in the book of Deuteronomy, telling them, *"This day I have set before you life and death, blessing and cursing. Therefore choose life"* (Deuteronomy 30:19). To take away choice is to take away freedom. So He gives you the freedom to choose what kind of person you want to be. Of course we know the kind of person He'd *like* for you to be, but the seed of choice planted inside your soul gives you the wonderful privilege to participate in the script of life—because He knows your journey there is just as important as the destination. In effect, that's what the blueprint is all about: establishing the steps you need to take to get where you need to go.

I find Twitter interesting because it kind of reveals a lot about people, especially celebrities. You get a chance to see what artists are really about, the way they dialogue, the stuff they talk about, the places they like to go. Some people I've tried to follow never talk about *anything*. I told my friend that I don't even want to follow this one dude anymore because when I get a tweet and I look at my phone, I want to see something inspiring. But he's like, "I'm at the mall and I'm buying something." That's not what I signed up for. I asked this same friend what kind of dude people would think I was from reading my tweets. He said people would conclude I was serious about the Word and interested in saying something meaningful. That doesn't affirm perfection—trust me!—but it gives me hope that I am becoming something greater than what I see right now. I talked earlier about embracing the non-sexies, and this is where it becomes especially important, in figuring out what the right choices are when so many options come flying at us on a daily basis. The non-sexies build those layers of maturity and wisdom, the spiritual essence that lifts us, so when you get into one of those difficult situations, it becomes clear to you what choice you're supposed to make. People who make the wrong choices do so because they have not put enough time in the inner work that comes from embracing the non-sexies. For me, this becomes particularly applicable when I think about Hollywood and my efforts to gain some traction in that industry. I have been going out to Hollywood since 1996; I've had deals with UPN, ABC, 20th Century Fox, Lions Gate. I'm talking about contracts signed, checks sent, actual money changing hands. Loot. But then it doesn't happen. Something falls through. I've been told "no" so many times, I can't even count them all. They're like, *Yeah, it's going to happen. We love you people! Boy, you guys are great!* And then, a bit later, *No. Not right now.* But you know what all those "nos" have been doing? They have been developing my inner work, giving me some lessons in contentment, some perspective, some maturity. So now, if God decides that I do get a "yes," hopefully I won't act a fool with it. See, God is not only preparing it for you, he's also preparing you for it. Almost made me shout!

Purge your soul of hatred.

When I was a young weed myself (funny), we didn't have money for those fancy lawnmowers and trimmers to keep our yard looking fresh. We had one of those old-school machines without a motor; you had to push it with some force over the grass to cut it. Sort of like two big wheels with blades in the middle. And the tool we used for the weeds in the yard? Me. I had to pull the weeds up with my hands. I hated that part of the job—so much that I never pulled them the right way. I'd rush through it, trying to get back in the house to watch cartoons, so I'd wind up only pulling the top part. Of course, after a few weeks it would come back again. Gertrude would say, "Boy, to get that weed right, you gotta make sure you get that root! If not, it'll be back real soon."

There is a weed that no matter how hard we try to pull, it keeps coming back. It may lay low for a while, hiding in the tall grass, silent for a few months or even a few years, but it never really goes away. Then in the ugliest ways, it will come back and keep growing and growing and once again defile the beauty of our world. Let's try to get to the root of the ugly weed: racism.

I wish Gertrude were here to see what just happened in America. She died before seeing a black man become president of her country. Whatever happens between the writing of these words and this book's coming out, this achievement by itself is something our elders would never in a million years have dared imagine, not in a country with our tainted history. For there can be no denying that history. When you look honestly at this country, you cannot talk about its greatness, its achievements, and its victories, without also talking about its cruelty and injustice, especially that done to a large group of individuals by the once legal and always bloody institution of slavery.

Slavery remains for America what steroids is to a major league baseball player's home-run record; it is the asterisk that causes discomfort whenever his achievements are named. Whenever our children read the blueprints about our nation, it will be there, lurking behind each sentence, screaming for justice, freedom, and equality. It will forever be the great mistake of the founding fathers of these United States.

Gertrude was born in 1910, a mere forty-five years after emancipation. She cleaned houses for white people and sewed clothes on the weekends for extra cash. I remember seeing her drop her head low when we walked into a department store and white women walked by. I didn't understand until I was older that, as a little girl, she was taught not to look white people in the eye. Thinking about it now, I can imagine her embarrassment at going to school with me and not understanding the white principal's explanation of her son's learning disability. Having only a fourth-grade education, her response was limited. And now the same White House that some of Gertrude's relatives might have helped build has a black man living inside it. She was born in 1910. It's now 2010.

Just recently, several African-American children in Philadelphia were not allowed to swim in a pool because their skin color made other swimmers uncomfortable. . . . Gertrude was born in 1910; it's now 2010. That perpetual stain, racial hatred, still stares us in the face. It is America's most damaging, longest-lasting weed. And if we aren't careful, it can wrap its tentacles around our necks and our hearts and squeeze the life out of us. That is why we all must struggle, during the process of lifescaping, to purge racial hatred from our souls. It is the only way we can make our way forward as individuals, as black people and white people and brown people, as a country.

If you read this and you know in your inner being that you have deep resentment, perhaps even hatred, for people whose skin, hair, or eyes look different from yours, your worship will never be pure, your soul will never be truly renewed, and your mind will never really be at peace until you deal with it. We all have it. Maybe the white officer wasn't being racist when he pulled me over for going 90 and didn't buy my story about being late for men's prayer night. And maybe the kids at the mall who held the door open for you at The Gap were not planning to rob you. Why continue to pray when you know you haven't done your part? Don't spiritualize those areas where you aren't living the way you know God calls you to live. Rather than waiting for Him to move others, move yourself!

> *You know.* When you pass over someone who is more qualified for someone who is less qualified because the first person's skin color makes you uncomfortable.

> *You know.* When your church doesn't make all members a part of her community.

> *You know.* When the thought of your daughter marrying outside her race or your son bringing home a young lady whose family's income is much lower than yours bothers you.

You know. When the black guy at work brings his blond, blue-eyed girlfriend to the office party and the whispering is louder than the music.

You know.

You know because when such things happen to you, you feel the embarrassment and isolation of being treated differently from those around you. Whether it's your black friends who tell jokes and share family stories that you can't relate to, coworkers who make you feel guilty for not having friends from the rough part of town, or tears on the face of the boy being interviewed on CNN about not being allowed to swim with his friends because of his skin color, you know. We all know. Because when it happens to us, we understand.

Everyone on some level has to be man or woman enough to admit what the light reveals—or else they will continue to live in darkness. *Living in darkness* . . . interesting.

We watched the faces of older African Americans the night of the election of the first black president. Some couldn't understand the tears, the lack of words, the overwhelming sense of finally belonging—when belonging once seemed utterly impossible. Gray-haired black men who grew up being called "boy," "coon," and "nigger," saw banners celebrating them as "American," "Citizen," and "We the People."

But then we hear the news reports of white supremacist groups threatening to assassinate the president because they refuse to have a black man lead the most powerful country in the world.

Weeds.

Still, for one night, for one brief moment, we took a deep breath. We cried. We danced. We remembered. And we finally believed

Not because we all agree with the president, not because we all think the same way he thinks, and not because we expect government policies or laws to make the world better overnight. But for the first time since we landed in England's Chesapeake Bay, France's New Orleans, or Spain's Florida, from the young to the old, we believed.

I have much gratitude for every man and woman—whatever their race or nationality—who sacrificed so that each of us can experience the hope of this great country. Many colors have died to make this nation a place where black men and white men, Jews and Gentiles, Protestants and Catholics, are free. Man, I wish I could have been there when Martin Luther King grabbed the mike and told America that this is everyone's country, that he wouldn't stop until everyone is free at last!

What if, when the last page is written on us as Americans, an asterisk appears next to each of the accomplishments of the twentieth century—putting a man on the moon, making advances in medicine and technology, greener cars, smarter phones—because we could never get the race thing right?

What if, when churches look back and marvel at all the social and political maneuvering they did for the sake of the common good, they realize they never really dealt with the race thing?

What if, when we die and stand before the Creator of the universe, we find out that what stood in the way of our receiving all the blessings God wanted to give us while we were on earth was our lack of love—a lack of real love that expressed itself in actions for those who looked different from us? There is no black heaven, no white heaven, no Hispanic heaven, no Asian heaven. Just one God, one family. And there will be no hate, no death; just Martin's dream—and, oh yeah, Gertrude will be there. *I can't wait!*

The system doesn't have to be your enemy.

After the Rodney King incident in 1991, the riots in Los Angeles gripped the entire country. It was the first time since the sixties that we saw racial tensions of that magnitude. Before that incident, the city had for years been filled with death and violence from infamous gangs like the Bloods and the Crips. After the riots, the city put together something called Project RLA (Rebuild LA). At least 74,000 jobs were supposed to be created and more than $6 billion invested in the middle of the riot zone over the next five years. After the announcement, a sense of hope was felt in the community—so much so, in fact, that the leaders of the gangs declared a peace treaty.

No more violence. Why? Because they were given hope.

One year later, with many buildings unfinished and a community still in ruin, Project RLA closed its doors. And with them were closed the doors of hope. The kids in the gangs felt lied to and grew frustrated. Gang violence rose again. Those kids felt let down, facing again the sort of disappointment many of them had experienced with their fathers. They felt anger and frustration over broken promises. Many came to see promises as things to be broken; they believed that promises made to them would never be kept.

As a young man, though I wasn't educated about politics, I hated the election season. Each year when running for office city officials would stop by the local churches and make their promises. Something about it seemed fake, like a hustle. And we never saw those guys after the election. Rarely if ever would you see any progress; so their words were worth as much as the gold watch being sold on the corner by Ned the wino.

I'm always amazed at children. Their innocence, the way they look at the world. Maybe you remember—I know I do—being young and playing with someone of a different color. You would play in the same mud, laugh at the same things, swing from the same rope because, through the eyes of a kid, fun has no color. You didn't care whether their hair was straight or nappy; even if they watched *The Brady Bunch* and you watched *Fat Albert*, fun has no color. It wasn't until your snuff-spitting grandmama told you that your friend was not like you that you even noticed. It wasn't until some stupid grown-up, uncomfortable with you playing with your colorless friend, made their skin an issue that you even cared. If only we could be like children again . . . "suffer the little children."

What this slow death of hope, this disappointment that the system seems to have always visited upon us, has too often done is create apathy and cynicism. In other words, people have checked out on life and no longer care. We can spot it right away all around us: *I don't vote because it won't make a difference—they all the same . . . It don't matter if I study or not 'cause ain't nobody tryin' to give a job/promotion/scholarship to a black man from the hood . . . Why should I work hard and break my back to make money for the white man—it ain't like he's sharing it with me!*

We all know somebody who walks around with the "forget them" chip on his shoulder. But I would offer that, even when the system seems to be stacked against us, there are always going to be ways to make it work *for* us. Black people have always been very clever at finding those things about ourselves that are attractive and maximizing them for our benefit. If a woman has pretty legs, she's going to wear things that accent them. We've always been able to take a suit that wasn't so expensive and put a fly tie with it or a different kind of shirt to put some soul to it. We need to take those same talents and apply them to this system that we feel is forever working against us. Find those areas that we shine in, figure out how we can take our talents and make that system more flavorful, more colorful, give it more swagger. If you are good at troubleshooting, always getting your boys to stop fighting and trippin', you might be able to take that same energy and bring it to the workplace, where you can resolve conflicts and troubles that arise. If you are good at thinking on your feet (like when you dial the wrong number and call the wrong female friend!) you might speak up or slip a note to your flustered boss the next time he needs help, rather than sitting there and silently enjoying his humiliation. The problem is that we don't want to work outside of our job description. We think, *I was hired to do this and that is all I'm going to do to get my check.* You've got to stop thinking of the system as an institution that was put there to hold you back. *I'm a black man and they're not going to let me have that job.* God has put you here to make a difference. Everywhere we go as people of color we've got to see that we're here divinely to make a difference. You are not just here to make money. And don't pay attention to what TV says it means to make a difference. We're led to believe that if you don't make a certain amount of money or you don't have a big audience that you can't make a difference. We've got to stop defining greatness as a number. If you can get your child through high school, college, and grad school, that's greatness. You have impacted the world by your sacrifices in this one child's life. We've got to start seeing that our reason for being on this planet has value that is bigger than a 9 to 5 or just being some black person in the hood. Whether or not the system or white folks or anyone else tells us, we have a reason for being here, and the Creator is waiting for us to see it. He loves the person you call white, and He loves you, my brown friend! You have to look over that wall of racism or sexism and see that your world is bigger than just this hood or this job. You are here to make a difference, so you need to find the thing that you were divinely created to contribute to the world. Stop complaining about the system, the white man, the job, the police, the hood, the government, the ex, the baby's daddy. Go find your difference.

Beware of the danger in the crossover.
In music, if a black artist gets radio play on a predominately white radio station, we define that as crossing over. Not until you cross over does your budget get really big and your profile really high. Only then do you have opportunities for magazine covers, a seat on a late-night talk show, or a chat with the women on *The View*. So what does every artist see as *the* goal? The acceptance of white people. And this creates an internal problem. Since those windows are only open for a few of the privileged, we constantly fight envy and jealousy within ourselves because of what being accepted by the white community brings—more success, more fame, more acceptance. Whether it's climbing the corporate ladder or getting a video on MTV (rather than BET), we see our legitimacy in terms of acceptance in the broader white world.

Most people of color can even remember having white friends in school who told us that, because we didn't talk as "black" or as "ghetto," we were not like "other" blacks. They were more comfortable around us if we were not as ethnic or "ghetto" in our dialogue and style. So many of us would tone down our "blackness" to be among those we considered the more influential and powerful friends in school. Whether in television or movies, music or sports, the value of their thumbs-up became what solidified us, affirmed us; it became the mark that we had arrived.

But what I've been most fascinated by over the past two years with the total collapse of our financial system is how that acceptance we were seeking in the mainstream world, that crossover magic, has been revealed as more like fool's gold. We thought they had all the answers, but behind closed doors they were taking a pill to help with the pill. *(I can't get that commercial out of my head!)* We need to be very careful with what we pursue because when we finally get behind the closed doors and start seeing the price that others pay, that their health and their minds and their psychological stability are often not well, we have to ask ourselves if we really want it. Are we willing to risk all that we have for that position or that acceptance? I bought a suit from Gucci, but the buttons on that Gucci suit broke just like the buttons on a J. Crew suit. You would think, *Man, this is a Gucci suit, it shouldn't break.* But even though the name Gucci is sewn inside the jacket, it has the same buttons as the other suit. We think it came from a different factory, but it was made in the same factory. Black people too often think of white people as being made in a different factory because they have the positions of power and influence. But like those buttons, we're all made in the same factory. And this economic collapse shows how much those buttons are breaking. The things we previously thought were strong and stable have been revealed as anything but strong and stable.

At the same time, in the black community we've got to stop putting out this sorry product that makes so many of us think we have to go over the bridge to get quality. The last-minute, not-thought-out product is not acceptable. And until we're willing to hold ourselves accountable, we're going to continue to see black people going over that bridge, seeking that acceptance, that crossover. They're going to keep going across the bridge until they start believing in our brand. The ones among us who are doing it right, we need to give them more applause and attention. But until the rest of us are seriously ready to do the inner work, we're just going to keep having panels and summits and conferences, and that's where it will end. There'll be the after parties and we'll all meet at the bar at the conference hotel that night, get blazed, and then hook up with a little conference "piece" and try to get some conference lovin'. Then the next day at the panel, everyone will be saying, "Black people need to do this, black people need to do that . . ."

So, if you're reading this and you want to know if there's

something you can do on a personal level to start the process of healing the world from this ugly weed of racism, I offer these thoughts. Whether you're black, white, Asian, Hispanic, purple, green, or blue, you should *crucify assumptions*. Stop assuming the worst of people based on the media, your community, your relatives, and your past. Since we have messed-up, stupid people in every color, let's assume and trust that God may have just placed an earthly treasure in your life to help pull this weed of racism up by the root so you both can plant new seeds together. We all need to move toward one another. Invite Becky and her husband, Brad, over for some of your sumptuous soul food. Learn how to laugh at some of their jokes. For those in other communities, discover that black people's history and heroes include more than MLK and Jay-Z. Be yourself around your black friends—when you're not it's uncomfortable for both of you. Last, for us all, *be intentional*. Don't wait for tragedies and accidents to bring this issue to the front page of your life.

Something amazing happened as soon as I finished writing this chapter. I asked a lady at the gym where I work out who happens to be white to read it and see if she could give me some constructive criticism. She is a very nice, well-educated woman. And her world is totally different from mine. I looked forward to learning from her criticism. After reading it, she sat with me and shared her honest views on the subject matter. Racism and slavery were used so much in the 2008 election that she was frustrated with what she called the race card. She believes that slavery has no affect on African Americans today, that we as black people are quick to scream injustice for things that we have full control over.

Basically, she said that we all have a choice about how our lives will end up. We sat for about thirty minutes sharing opposing views when we heard a loud crash outside the gym. We ran outside and saw two cars had just collided. One was a pickup truck; the other was a car with a white couple inside it. They looked to be in their sixties and were a bit shaken up. Their front bumper was hanging off, keeping them from moving the car out of the middle of the intersection. Along with an older African-American man, I went over to check on them, then we disconnected the front bumper so they could move the car.

As the gentleman and I were carrying the bumper to the curb, the older white woman, fresh off being in a wreck, found enough strength to yell from her passenger window, "Hey! Don't you two run off with our bumper!" The gentleman and I, each looking frustrated and offended, found the inner strength to turn and gently assure her that we were *not* on our way to the junkyard for some quick cash. The lady from the gym stood on the corner, watching and overhearing all of this. When I walked back toward her, she said to me softly, *"I get it now."*

In real time, she had seen the topic come to life before her eyes. Of course, that the lady in the car was in her sixties and from the South might make some see it as an isolated event. But you have to be a flat-out cynical person to believe that what happened was just some coincidence. It was a chance for two of God's children to watch a painful part of our society come alive, so we both could learn and feel life together, if only for that one brief "wreck." Sometimes those crashes in life force us to confront the things that separate us. Some never get to that point because they "hit and run" (*there I go again!*). They see the problems with race, add to the problems of race, but never stick around long enough to learn what the wreck was intended to teach them, to be made aware of the things that such "accidents" can show us. But if crashes are what it takes to bring us together, let it be: *Boom!*

Chapter Six

IF YOU'RE SINGLE, MAKE SOME NOISE!

Okay, so there's just you. Your goals, your career, your crew, your prospects, and your God. All together, chillin'. Before the house, the apartment, the kids, the boyfriend, the wedding, the night you crossed over with your frat brothers, there's that pivotal point of asking your heart, "Who am I, really? What do I really like? Do I *want* to change for someone else? Is my soul mate right now, somewhere, finishing this sentence and completing my thoughts?"

Yes, I remember the single life well. The mixture of joy and sadness; contentment and compromise; success and . . . well, you feel me. And I also know the single archetypes: There is the "Christian" single—the one with the dedication to her God and everything and everyone in her life must align themselves with that commitment. There's the "club and church" single— the one who blends a little bit of both in his "life drink." These singles live a single life "shaken but not stirred," wanting a person who loves God, but they want to help God pick out the details. You even have the "power" single—master's degree,

condo, convertible, maybe goes to church Christmas and Easter. Loves brunch with friends, knows all the fresh fashions, can
take or leave a relationship, and from time to time, doesn't
mind someone coming by and "tuning up" the engine—but
don't get too serious, or you're out. Then there's the "desperation" single who needs to be saved, rescued from all of life's
misery and pain. She jumps headfirst into anyone who smiles
during offering, compliments what she has on, or asks, "Is this
seat taken?"

"Girl! The Lord sent me my husband on the train!"

No, boo-boo, he just needed a seat. The desperation for her
to be loved suffocates any contender or just plain old friend. Too
available, too needy, and the weight to be wanted is a space only
God was created to fill.

In my research, I found many seasons of singlehood. Those
who were truly content but were open if love walked through
the door. Those who found family and friends as their source of
satisfaction. Those whose experiences were so painful, they
numbed themselves to anything and anyone who required any
type of emotional investment. Even those who were deeply in
love with . . . themselves, to the point where no one else could
even compete—an abnormal threesome between "me, myself,
and I." Whether happy or hiding, satisfied yet searching, the single man or woman in the ever-eroding landscape of marriage
and love has the opportunity more than ever to make a great and
powerful difference in this cold and heartless world. How beautiful it would be if, before we enter into covenants with others,
we got right the covenant with ourselves and the God who created this love thing. Till death do us part. That's what we're going to do in this chapter—construct a blueprint for singles to
help you work on that "self" covenant. And whether they're
friends, family, or that special someone, don't be surprised if everyone begins to notice that new and glowing you.

Gray is the loneliest color. Don't let it beat you down.

Single: a variety of many different hues. You ask twenty single people to paint their picture of it and you get twenty different colors. One person's palette reveals a journey, bright yellows and reds, the excitement and the discovery of one's life. Another brush paints a warm violet, a scene in between dusk and dawn. A place called "meantime." Then there is one color in particular that paints an image close to my heart, familiar with my yesterday. A metaphorical easel that I found many singles share. Dark blues, smoke grays, the color of night; it is by far the greatest challenge, one of life's unsolvable mysteries, the "impetus magnus" (that means it's big!): loneliness.

I remember it well. It still even tries to stop by from time to time. It is a paralyzing emotion, one that will gnaw at the door of your one-bedroom apartment until the early sunrise. It causes you to make choices you regret the next day. Loneliness—that condition where you find yourself the odd person at banquets, and always feeling left out of the jokes all the couples laugh at. Sometimes there's not a sermon, a song, or an inspirational word from the preacher that can cut the cords of silence you experience when facing its brutal assaults alone at night.

It's very difficult to write about this because I understand that words fade, loving who you are fades, taking yourself on a date fades (quickly!). Invitations to Thanksgiving dinners at your sister's house with her perfect church-fan-looking family can tick you off and make you want to throw a turkey leg at somebody! But you smile anyhow, staring at the clock and praying that the old pimp-dressed, "Jerome in da house"–looking brother that just strolled in with cornrows is not the surprise your brother-in-law said he had with your name on it.

Again, if there's any encouragement I can share, loneliness does not discriminate. Married people can feel its choking cords in a room filled with people; on a stage in front of thousands;

waiting in a dressing room alone for hours; in a hotel room in Budapest, thousands of miles away from home. For some, it's lying next to your spouse who confessed weeks earlier to an extramarital affair; it's at the tomb changing flowers of a mother who tried to fight but finally lost to cancer. I assure you, single brother or sister, when the heavy hand of loneliness falls, the entire human race is her victim.

When loneliness creeps into the corridors of our brokenness, I have learned that it manifests itself differently between the sexes. For some women, loneliness reveals itself through overeating; food becomes that friend. Or it may produce a bitter and negative undertone in their attitudes (which can run away a man in a heartbeat, ladies). Or they become motherly in all of their relationships, positioning themselves as the entire community's self-appointed counselor, camouflaging their need to be helped in the attire of helping everybody else. Or there's the "I'll run you off on my terms, because you're gonna leave me anyway" woman. Her strength is a mirage in hurt's desert. And we all know the workaholic—she's slowly dying inside as she approaches the podium to receive another award for her accomplishments at the firm.

For men, loneliness can be much more destructive and dangerous. Women also can become engaged in some self-mutilating behavior, but a man can become like an animal in his pursuit to fill the empty space. Drugs, alcohol, whatever "friend" he can find to stay over, he pursues. We are hunters by nature, and we will hunt in an attempt just to be praised and acknowledged by another human being. That's why we perform at the office or in the world—to hear the applause of another. But empty rooms can't speak back. Sports cars can't kiss the side of your face in the parking lot, and money may be able to dress a man up, but it can't tell him how good he looks. So loneliness now pulls its biggest and oldest rabbit out of the hat. Sex. For a man, loneliness and sexual desires often go hand in hand. I've learned from women that they may have sexual desires, but it's not the driving force of their emptiness. It's more about companionship. A friend to confide in, spend a nice summer day with, and feel the fulfillment that hanging with your girlfriends can't compare to. But a man will watch a flick if he can't sleep; he'll call someone he has no plans of spending forever with. Women can go longer be by themselves. Period. A man needs to be mirrored back; unfortunately, it's hard for him to keep his clothes on while he's doing it.

Don't live and love in fear.

Because the burden of loneliness can dislodge your instincts from time to time and begin to create a fearful panic, you can begin to lower your standards. And this is where the trash comes in.

You know that marriage is the right thing to do. You were raised knowing the difference between right and wrong. But you allow this boy, good-looking, smooth, with lots of dough . . . whatever! Like I said, you allow this boy (and loneliness) to talk you into things your spirit says aren't right. But because you've been in this spot for sooo long, you adjust to his standards. He tells you he loves you, wants to be with you forever, and will give you everything, and you don't have to wait until marriage to get it. Or he doesn't say any of that, he just slowly starts to do it. He slowly starts to give you those "married things": He pays the car note for April. He does it again in May. You ask him questions, but because he says, "Don't worry about it" (and plus your money was already a little funny), you let him. He spends the night more . . . and more. He starts to leave clothes over, more . . . and more. You're cool with it because you lie to yourself and say, "Well, at least I know where he is at night. . . ." Whatever. After car notes, rent bills, Gucci bags, Prada shoes, and four birthdays, he has done a successful job of giving you all of the external benefits of marriage, with no commitment. Good job, playa!

Or you, my queen, start to do the same. You give him a nice home-cooked meal, more . . . and more. You let him keep your car while you're at work, more . . . and more. You let him stay over, MORE AND . . . then, you give him your body. Not because you were ready, not even because you were feeling him like that. But because in your mind you know men like what they like, so you give. And loneliness takes a temporary backseat, and watches you drive down "pretend street," and you feel the gas will never run out. But it always does. And for some of you, this isn't your first time stuck on the side of the road (with little Tray-Tray crying back in the car seat, next to loneliness).

There was a girl on Twitter once who asked me, "Why is it such a big deal to wait to have sex until you get married?" She said, "Why not test drive the car before you buy it?" Wow. What baby girl doesn't realize is that the test drive never ends; in your soul, your mind, you take the ride with you to the next car—and the miles keep adding up.

We'll come back to this, but can I be a big brother (no short jokes!) to both sides for a minute?

My single soldiers, I know you get so tired of the relationship/dating thing, so everybody is compromising these days. The "So, where you from; you come here often?" cycle goes on for so long, that you no longer dig deep in your relationships. When you walk on the beach, you see oyster shells buried in the sand. If you pick one up, I guarantee you won't find a pearl inside, because oysters can only make pearls in the deep part of the ocean. So if you just want any old shell, there are many just lying on the shore. But to get one with a pearl, you have to go deep. Single men should see women not as something convenient or lying around waiting to be picked up, but as someone who has to be searched for, sought out. For that pearl, he should have to go deep. But ladies, why should he . . . if your shell is always open?

This is not a chapter on sex, but there is no way to talk about the tree (loneliness) and not speak about *all* of the fruit it produces.

Again, if you are a single woman reading this chapter, sex may not be the biggest issue in your life. But if you are a single man, striving to live a strong, Godly, celibate life, sex is likely something that you need help with. Single women, you need to hear this because I hear you say that it can be frustrating and confusing to you why sex always has to be the determining factor in a relationship with a man. Well, sister, sugar, sweet daughter, if I could fix that in this book, Jesus would be my middle name. We can't deny that the fall in the garden created a wedge between the two of us, boy and girl, but until the real Jesus comes, if you want a good, healthy relationship with a guy that is either romantic or not, young lady, you hold the key. It is your honesty with your male friend that will be the strength of your time together. Since sex proba . . . ba . . . um . . . Since sex WILL be on his mind before it's on yours, you have to set the parameters. Even for those of you out there who are just "friends," never forget the power of human attraction. God made us that way, and many friends have ended up butt naked the next morning wondering how they got there because of one movie night too many. And really, fellas, we are the leaders. I know we have a generation of men who haven't been taught to have self-control, and how to stop a situation when it gets too heated—and even if you've been taught, it's just so doggone hard! But we're killing each other and producing generations of hurt between women and men—and the kids we continue to have that we weren't ready for suffer and we still end up alone . . . but now with extra luggage. And I don't know if you've flown lately, but you now have to pay for extra luggage. Mistakes cost.

So we see the fruit that loneliness bears: bad choices, bad attitudes, broken hearts, cold hearts, lowered standards, destructive cycles—emotionally and physically.

When loneliness causes you to lower your bar, to treat someone's daughter/son and yourself like GM stock, you have now become its servant, and it is your Lord. You can no longer brush off the power that you have given to it. It engages everything you do. The reality is there. Don't deny it; here's what you have to do: *Visit, but don't move in.* Yes! I like that for many things in life: Visit, but don't move in. Acknowledge that it can be a hard mountain to climb, but it's not impossible. Don't dwell there. Don't get stuck in it. You have climbed many more Mt. "Impossibles" and made it!

I know both sides might look at me now after fourteen years of being married and feel like I am not able to speak about being single in a way they can truly relate to, that I can sympathize but not empathize. So I called some friends over one night and had a real straight talk about this topic. It was great! I wanted to keep it raw and real so you wouldn't hear my words but theirs. I changed the names so their business wouldn't be all out there.

Shari	26, single, but has a longtime boyfriend
Lauren	26, single, in and out of a drama-filled relationship
Debrah	34, divorced, three kids
Henry	32, single, has a girlfriend, has commitment issues
David	35, married
Leon	36, married, but his eyes are single
Kirk	What is the biggest challenge in being single right now?
Debrah	Celibacy. How do you go from having sexual relationships, having the memory of it to now being single, divorced, but you can't divorce the thought?

Kirk   Well, hopefully you learned from your past relationship that the sex, no matter how good or bad, ain't enough to keep a relationship. See, it's when we forget the reality of the pain these relationships bring that we get caught up in that deadly cycle of repeating them over and over again. So as hard as it may be to know what something tastes like, burning off the "calories" of the experience just ain't worth it. And Debrah, that can no longer be driven by your feelings, but by the truth. You owe yourself that.

Lauren   Mine is keeping these married men off of me!

Shari   Girl, you're right! It's like they sniff out the young single girls to be their little treats to buy things for because the wifey ain't doin' it for them anymore.

Kirk   So it's that bad?

Shari   Yes! You feel as a single woman nowadays that you almost have to hide your status because that's who comes after you mostly. And the down-low brothers scare me to death!

Kirk   Well, just know that if you ever become his little treat, he will always desire many flavors, because that's what the flesh likes—variety. He will end up disposing of you like he does his wife. What about you, Henry?

Henry   Just the pressure from her and her family about marriage. I don't want to feel pressured. Her grandmother told me the other day, "You know, you can date too long, Sugar." I said, "Yes, ma'am," but in my heart I feel like we'll know when it's right, and plus I'm trying to get my paper right first.

Lauren   But when is too long? I don't want to be your girlfriend forever—that's whack!

Henry   But don't stick around trying to make that happen either.

Kirk   But Henry, you gotta understand that the greatest symbol for love is commitment. Love that isn't committed is lust. You should at some point want to give her the assurance that you are here for the duration of life. Is that scary?

Henry   H*** yeah! I don't know nobody who is married and faithful or happy. My folks didn't stick it out and . . .

Kirk   That's it, Henry! It's the fear of "what if." Nobody can answer "what if." What if you got into a car wreck and were paralyzed the rest of your life? What "girlfriend" is gonna stick around to wipe spit from the corner of your mouth, or change your bedpan? A girlfriend won't. But a woman who was given the greatest gift of commitment, trust, provision, and felt like a queen in her home and in front of your children together will remember her vows. In sickness and health. If she was never given the gift of vows, what's there to remember?

Lauren   So Kirk, when is it "too long" in dating?

Kirk   When you look like the picture, but you still don't have the frame.

Lauren   Huh?

Kirk   [Laughs] When everything about your relationship looks like the ones that are committed and married, that reflect the picture on the wall of a unit. A team. A family. Vacations together, buying things together, your mom's for Christmas this year and his next year, and you've done this so much it's a routine. But no one ever asks, "When do we get off the ride?"

            You feel it; you know it, and you're not honest with the

other person about what you feel. So you stay, but you stay frustrated. If you know that you're at a different place in your life from the other person, not being honest for the sake of not being lonely is lying, to them and to you. And as a man I can promise you, he knows when you're the one. He knows because he includes you in his future plans. He knows because staying in with you is what he looks forward to. He knows because he's just as fulfilled if your clothes never come off. He knows because he wants all his female friends to meet you. He knows because he's troubled if a thought that enters into his mind doesn't include you. He knows if he just enjoys your company, or if he wants to wifey you. It's not taking him another slice of your mama's sweet potato pie to figure out if you're the one.

Debrah   What about honesty? That was my problem in my last marriage. He wasn't honest.

Shari   Girl, men aren't honest.

David   Not true. Men want to be honest, but we don't want to hurt you, and some truth will. So how do you become honest and not see you hurt at the same time?

Lauren   Think about how the same hurt would make you feel!

Henry   But it's not just about you. We don't want to deal with how the truth makes us feel about ourselves. Because some stuff, we can't believe we did either!

David   And a man needs to know he has a safe place to fall.

Debrah   But if you love someone, it can't last without truth.

Shari   How would you feel if women responded to secrets like men do?

Leon   Y'all do! [Laughs]

So the journey continues. . . . It continues because Venus and Mars do exist, and men and women can never seem to get the planets to come together. Wouldn't it be great if you could just learn the life lessons and move on? To stop trying to find yourself in another person or thing and embrace what's supposed to be one of the greatest seasons in your life? Because every lesson not learned will be repeated. Why can't we learn and move on? Maybe because you put too much on the external? The looks, the size, the income bracket. Maybe, as a single, you're no longer looking for depth, now it's just hype. Tammy was not the first beautiful woman I dated, but when she spoke she had a voice. She was a thinker; actually, she's brilliant! She even toned my clothes down; they were entirely too bright and colorful before I met her. After I asked her to marry me, she said to me, "Babe, I know you got some loose strings out there because you told me and I'm not a fool. Before I move down there I'm asking you to make sure that every other 'account' is closed and that no other woman can come up to me and tell me something that I don't already know from you." Like a little-bitty man in love, I did it. If I would have just married for the outside, the external, I would have missed a divine opportunity to go deeper.

Get out of yourself.

As I said before, I had to grapple with a lot of selfishness in the early days of my marriage and my family. I had that only-child syndrome in so many areas of my life. But I had to get over it pretty quickly when I had children. If you are going to have healthy children and a healthy home, there's a sense of invasion that children bring with them. They develop a sense of selflessness in you if you are an engaged parent. If you're not, then they are just going to frustrate you because they keep knocking on that door, entering the room at times when you don't want them to. But they were created to knock on that door. So you can't get mad at them for doing something that's natural, to want to be in your presence, to soak up your essence. That's what they do.

But for singles, those who live alone without children, a little more work must be put in to achieve that all-important selflessness. I think for singles to get healthy, what you have to do is *serve*. By serving, you start doing that inner work; you get out of yourself and start working on the non-sexies. You have to find lives that you can help change. Lives that may not be able to pay you back. One of the most misplaced populations in our society is the elderly. Perhaps there's an opportunity there for you to help others. How we treat older people is ridiculous; they have all that knowledge, but when they can't do for themselves we just put them away somewhere. If that makes you uncomfortable, maybe you would do better with children. It won't take you long to find a group that helps children where you can volunteer. If you can't find one, maybe you could even start your own. We were created to serve. When you look at God's Word and consider His template for humanity, all throughout the text it talks about serving. Christ said in Matthew's gospel, *The greatest among you must be your servant* (Matthew 23:11). Don't take the hot position; take the lowly seat. Jesus moved among the people, talking to the adulterers and the killers. It is about denying self for the sake of someone else. When servants can see life as bigger than themselves, that's when they can also find fulfillment.

You can tell when a person isn't healthy because even when they think they're serving, all they talk about is the many things that they do. Because they need validation. *Oh girl, I was over there doing that thing for charity. I'm so tired.* But when you're coming from a healthy place, you don't have to do that. Unhealthy people talk about themselves because they need it; they have to have it because their foundation isn't right. But healthy people have a glow. My wife tells me that the times when I turn her on the most is when I'm helping the kids. Not when I'm in the gym and coming home all sweaty in my little tights, or on the stage doing my thing. No, helping with the kids. For a man, that's one of the most non-sexy things we could be doing, like how can that be sexy? But when we do the things that we think are sexy, that's when it's not sexy. (Since she told me that, my kids are almost white now cause I've bathed them so much!) There's something about being healthy; it just creates this inner fire inside of you that you can't even explain.

There's a purpose for the pain.

Too often singles fail to embrace the beauty of the season. You've allowed the frustration, the disappointments, the pain of being single blind you from the joys of being single. And whatever painful times you've gone through or still may be going through, never forget that there is *always* a purpose for the pain.

One day my daughter Kennedy was complaining about this severe pain in the joints of her legs. She told me that the pain was unbearable and she needed to go to the emergency room. Now anyone who knows Kennedy KNOWS that she is Miss Drama Queen. She is twelve and a daddy's girl to the limit. Knowing my baby, I suggested, "Boo, I think those may be growing pains you're feeling in your joints. That happens when you're going through a growth spurt." (I'm going somewhere with this!) Because my baby can't wait to grow up, she got ex- cited and totally forgot about the pain when she heard that it was connected to her growth. And she hasn't mentioned the pain since.

You have to see the pain and struggle of being single as connected to something much bigger than what you are going through right now—just make sure the pain is not self-induced! If bad choices are becoming a habit for you, then you can't include God on that one; He's not wanting you to kick your own self in the butt time after time to teach you that "butt kicking" hurts. But God can and does use pains that can grow you into a strong, healthy individual, so that if and when someone comes into your life, they don't *make* your life, they come alongside and *add* to your life. If that's the case, then it's worth the hell, the loneliness. As long as you're growing, it's worth the growing pains.

If you are single and have gone through the process of being happy and whole, the world is your canvas. That sounds good, doesn't it! Paul in the Bible was talking to his young homie Timothy, and told him family is a necessary distraction and a man or a woman who doesn't take care of their family is worse than a sinner. So with no legitimate boundaries or distractions in your way, you're like a star athlete in college with NFL teams lining up, begging you to help make their team champions. Your value is so important to this team. And I ask of you right now, to please forgive those who have made single life look like a death sentence. I know that some in the church have even made being single look like a sin, like something must be wrong with you, when in reality many single people are seeing the infidelity and unhappiness in the lives of many married people and *that*, my friend, is the real sin.

One of the worst tricks a single can play on herself is to think that all married people walk around all smiling and jumping through the tulips thanking the Big Wedding Singer on High for this glorious gift of a person to spend your old prune-eating, apple-preserve-making, Metamucil-drinking life with. There are many, and I mean *many*, in and out of the church who would love for a piano falling out of a high-rise to take their significant other to that mansion in the sky! Do not look at every house on your street and assume that it's a home paid off and fully furnished; can somebody say "foreclosure"? Marriage doesn't necessarily make *you* better, but your strong, secure, spiritually aware life should help make marriage better. Single people, understand that marriage is not two halves making one whole; rather, it's two wholes making a new whole. In the divine equation, the math is different from what we expect. The kingdom work that single people can do is not filled with the guilt and conviction that a lot of married people, including myself, deal with. Many times I feel like I'm leaving my family uncovered, or how at any time, my music has the potential to become the "other woman." Don't get me wrong; learning from couples that model a healthy, Godly marriage is dope! We all need to be around strong, loving blueprints to give us a map of how to accomplish this thing that is becoming more extinct day by day. But don't gaze in frustration because of what you think you don't have. Just remember being single is great, being married is great, but they are both *hard* work.

Single is the season where you study you. You nurture good relationships and feed the part of you that's learning, falling, and becoming. It's where you find out what you like in the arts; is it Bach? Miles? Etta? What styles of food do you like? (Ladies! This is so important that you learn this now, because men *hate* hearing, "I don't know" when it's time to order! Pick something, please!) Test your depths as a coworker in God's plan for mankind. Become a missionary, travel internationally, change your major two, three, four times; intentionally become friends with the opposite sex. Learn how to spot "game." Ask guys how to pick up on a guy who thinks he's the gift to all the girls in the choir. This time in life can be a beautiful blessing, a gift from God. But if you despise the gift, you lose the glow. You lose the zest for life. But oh, my friend, I see you as a powerful partner in changing this scary, lost world. You can go places I can't go. You can do things I can't do. I need you on my team. And bring your crew!

You must have like-minded friends.

Don't live this part of your life on your own. Every soldier has to be part of an army. And like a soldier in battle, your fellow soldiers will be the key to your survival. When bullets are flying over our heads, no one can be caught sleeping on the job. Lives are lost when soldiers let their guard down in war. Hear me well, you *must* have like-minded friends. If they're not like-minded, they will sap all of your energy, chasing knuckle-headed dudes, having you doing stupid stuff with them, sitting in the car all night in front of a girl's house she thinks he's messing with, just silly little kid stuff. You gotta have soldiers! You don't need many; get you one good friend who will tell you when you're tripping, and tell you when you're doing a good job. And serve God with all your heart; He won't let you down. He, too, is a close friend. He has great plans for you. To give you hope and a future.

And last, again I beg of you, from my own experience, remember the rabbit that loneliness pulls. I say it again because I would have given anything to have had someone tell me while I was single that sex destroys *everything*. I don't care what sexy song is on the radio, or what the plot of the next *Sex and the City* will be, but I can tell you, singles, you are setting yourselves up if you don't guard your mind, and your "one time only" gift from the pitfalls of this flesh. Single sex gives you an unrealistic perspective of sex. Y'all are not having sex, y'all are having a show. You even have angry married people who brought too much "show" luggage into their homes. You've heard them, "Stay single as long as you can, because you stop having sex, or it's boring when you get married." That's the "show" talking. Married sex isn't boring; no, married sex is real.

If Tom Cruise jumped out of a plane onto another plane in real life, he'd probably die. And most of the stunts are done by doubles anyway. But there are no "doubles" in real life, especially when it comes to marriage and sex. The director doesn't yell, "Cut!" No one comes along to stand in for you. There's no background music. And the scene where the elevator stops and you rip each other's clothes off while kissing each other's faces like they're dessert pretty much never happens; the scene during the ending credits with the two of you on the beach, the sun setting, the water brushing her hair over his chiseled chest and the two of you making hot passionate love all night until the morning . . . PLEASE! The salt water makes your skin dry, if your wife is a sister she's gonna complain about getting her hair wet, the sand doesn't feel good going up your drawers, and somebody has to go to work in the morning! And oh yeah, Tray-Tray had an accident at school and you've got to get your butt up off the beach and take him some new pants 'cause the third graders are calling him "pee-pee boy." *That's* real life. And if you've done nothing but perform all your single life, you're going to be disappointed when the movie ends. Your life is bigger than sex, bigger than chasing relationships, bigger than crying alone because loneliness has once again attacked your heart. Don't give it that much credit. Don't cheapen this moment with one night. And, just like Kennedy, get excited about the growth that is in store. And again, ladies, find out now what kind of food you like, so y'all can get to the movie! Then later, make him go home.

Chapter Seven

THE BLUEPRINT FOR MY SOLDIERS

By now it is clear that I am a man, a black man. I am a Christian. I am a father. I am a husband. And as strange as it sounds to me, I am someone's son. I love music. Indeed, I am passionate about all kinds of music—jazz, rock, classical, hip-hop, and gospel. I hope it's also clear that I love my family. I love my wife. I love my children. And I love working with other people's children; sometimes I think I'm living out a childhood I never really enjoyed. This is who I am. But I am also hurting. And my pain comes from a very familiar source. My brothers. My soldiers.

If you don't mind, in this chapter I'd like to discuss something very important to me—black men. As far back as I can remember, I've always been fascinated with the presence the black man has—how a room stops when he enters, how there always seems to be tension when the police drive down the street, even when we are just standing around minding our own business. Admittedly, my fascination probably comes from the fact that, when I was growing up, there was never a man in the house. So whenever a black man was around, I'd stare at him like I was looking at an alien from another planet—in awe and with great excitement.

The first thing we need to say to men is this: *You're right*. You have been done wrong. You're right; the system did fail you. You're right; there were men who were supposed to be there to give you a baton that was not dropped, that was not dirty, that was not contaminated. You need to hear another man say it to you, *You are right*. You are hurt. Your hurt is justifiable. Now I'm about to ask you to do something that may be painful, brother. It may be out of your comfort zone. But if you believe that every bad, ugly thing does have a purpose connected to it, I'm challenging you at this very moment to gather enough strength to look past this wall you have built for decades; the wall that reads hurt. I am daring you to just get a little bit of strength, not even for the rest of your life but for today. If I can get you to turn off the soapbox and just take a pain time-out. I'm not saying let it all go today. But just give it a time-out and look over this wall you've built. Maybe it was built for you, maybe you helped build it. But if you can just peek over it for a moment, if you can look over to the other side, you will see that your life is not over. You will see that there's something bigger you were created for. If not, you would be dead by now.

But now that I hopefully have convinced you to come with me over that wall, I need to be honest with you. I have to tell the truth here, to talk about how much the rest of us are now hurting by your absence. As brothers, we have always placed value in those who "keep it real, who keep it 100," so let me be 100 with you in this chapter. It may not be pretty or feel good, but I'm going to say what must be said. Let me talk to my soldiers.

To be honest, it has been difficult lately to find a community of brothers with whom I share the same passions, morals, and goals. Not because of some economic or social reason, but simply because it's getting harder and harder to find men who want to grow, who want to be better than they are. I celebrate the powerful black man in society—the father, the leader, the professional. I wish the media showed more of him. But for the moment I'm concerned about what I *do* see, about what needs to change. Whether it's the married man who can't see past the girl at the other table, or the one who desires to be just a churchgoer rather than an ambassador for change in the world around him. Because my past can no longer be an excuse for not being the father and husband I need to be, I won't make excuses anymore. And I'm tired of those who do. Values seem to be a thing of yesterday; the notion of manhood is fading as fast as Milli Vanilli in the nineties. It makes me think of Michael Jackson's song "Man in the Mirror." Even though that song is almost twenty years old, I believe it describes the challenge faced by my brothers and society.

Perhaps some in academia would tell me to tread lightly on this topic because I'm not educated enough about the economic and social impact of slavery, segregation, and discrimination against the black male in the workforce, as well as the hopelessness these things have created in the psyche of a group of displaced human beings. So perhaps I should stay in my lane, just play the piano and sing songs to make us feel better.

My response? *No.* If you don't remember, I'll tell you again. I was raised in the South. We were called "nigger" so much it became part of our self-comprehension. I was adopted by a sixty-four-year-old woman with a fourth-grade education. She cleaned houses for white people for $10 a week. My father was the worst excuse for a man who ever lived. No interest, no involvement. I have no high school diploma, was labeled ADHD—or else just dumb—by mostly white schools, and I was a teenage father, with no hope of escaping. No role models, no after-school programs, a sister in prison along with a grandfather and a stepfather. All in prison, same time, same state. All I had was a genuine love and acceptance for the faith instilled in me as a child, a faith that gave

me the choice either to be who God says I am or to use excuses
to continue the same pattern I saw being lived by all the men in
my life, in and out of the church. I chose the former.

So no, I haven't taken formal classes in African-American
studies; and I wasn't involved in the sixties marches. But I speak
from life. A life filled with pain because I had no man to teach
me how to love or say, "I'm sorry." I speak from the heart of a
fatherless son. I speak from the lessons of thousands of boys I've
been blessed to work with across this country, boys I've shared
my story with and helped to work through theirs. I speak confidently about a host of men who look like me, sound like me, cry
like me, bleed like me—men whose ancestors got off the same
boat as mine. I say confidently and with much conviction: *It's
time to stop with all the d*mned excuses!*

Yes, we have to work harder than most. Yes, there are hurdles
we have to jump higher to get over. And yes, a lot of the pain
and frustration we feel is justified. But how many of our sons
must continue to pay the price for our anger at the world we
chose to bring them into? Nobody raped us; no woman pulled a
gun out and threatened to kill us if we didn't have sex with her.
These boys and girls are suffering because we're angry. They
didn't ask to be here; and they receive the anger that prevents us
from caring for them, loving them, and raising them to stop the
cycle of anger that was placed on us.

Research shows and professionals agree that a child who has
his daddy in his life has a better chance of winning. Of winning
against drugs, against gangs. Whatever the contest, such a boy
has a much better chance of winning it. How can a father who
has failed at most things in his life not want success for the one
thing he *can* succeed at—raising his own son? No amount of
baby mama drama should stop a man from doing his best to
have an ongoing relationship with the child he helped create. If
your clothes and apartment look better than your child, you are

a sorry father. If your girlfriend's kids get more time from you than your own kids, you are a sorry father. If you can't be bothered to adjust your schedule for something involving your own flesh and blood, you are a sorry father.

After the Columbine shootings, Columbia University did a study to find out how being raised in a single-parent home headed by a mother or in a home with both parents affects a child's involvement with alcohol, drugs, and violence. The report revealed that a child raised in a single-parent home by his mom is 30 percent more likely to be involved with alcohol, drugs, or violence than a child in a home with both parents. Now it doesn't take an expert to know that's *very* high. But here's what tripped me out—a child raised in a two-parent home with a poor relationship with the father is *68 percent* more likely to get involved with alcohol, drugs, or violence. *That's crazy!*

I believe that the greatest mark made on this planet will not be by scientists or doctors or even political revolutionaries. That mark will be made by the father who offers simple, day-to-day encouragement: *Did you do your homework? . . . Don't talk to your mother that way. . . . Be home by your curfew. . . . It doesn't matter whether you win or lose, but . . .* That's the role of one who's often imitated but never duplicated. Father.

I'll never forget being eighteen years old and a new father. It was scary, embarrassing, and depressing to have this beautiful child and no idea in the world what to do. I also remember the anger I felt toward my son's mother for getting pregnant in the first place, toward this beautiful baby for crying and crying all night, for forcing me to get a car with a backseat, and for all the dreams that had to be put in the trash because of this new reality. For a long time, I fathered out of fear and anger. I was there; I was never absent, but at times I was *just* there. This was not a happy place for me. This was not my plan for life. The diapers messed with what little money I had; and the baby *always* needed formula. I was not prepared for the responsibility. But I soon learned that I could not stand in front of people every Sunday and live a life that was a lie. My parenting had to match what I preached. I hated fakes and I didn't want to be one. So I chose to take steps and to ask questions; and I prayed to God to give me what I didn't naturally have—a father's skill set.

There is no other way to say it except clearly and honestly. Our lack of fathering is creating a generation of malnourished kids. Kids who don't know how to take life seriously, who don't take education seriously, who watch us live foolishly. Like us, they go from relationship to relationship and end up having children. Kids having kids—just like us. The problem is not all them big homie; *we* are a lot of it. So in the interest of healing the black community, I offer here a transformative blueprint for African-American men, my soldiers, my kings in the making. These are the first steps down a long path for my brothers, but I want you to know that I will be there with you, working hard on my own stuff. We have no other choice but to take this walk together. Our children are waiting for us, our women are waiting—indeed, our country is waiting. Come with me.

We need to tell our children we are sorry.
We are sorry for putting life's problems on them, for burdening them with our painful past. We need to ask their forgiveness for allowing gangs to fill the void that should have been filled by daddy. We need to apologize to our daughters for not protecting them from guys who should have had to go through us before they could get close to their hearts. We need to tell their mothers we are sorry for living in anger against them. We need to tell them that whatever the drama, it took two to create it.

I guarantee you, based on my life, that when we acknowledge what we didn't know, we free God to come transform what the professionals can't, what society can't, what political and social movements can't. Because everything physical and visible is first preceded by what is invisible and spiritual. I say that a lot because I don't want you to forget it! Some scholars may not agree with that, but I'm living proof.

This is not a perfect world, and this is definitely not a perfect country. But it's where I am. It's what my life looks like. So what am I going to do to move away from anger and toward peace? Anger that does nothing but hinder me and everyone connected to me. I choose to change what I can and to use what I can't as fuel to make me stronger. And I choose to view life through the lens of forgiveness. To forgive others, and even to forgive myself; you need to forgive others not only for their sake but also for yours. You have dreams. You have a future. And you have children who love and need you.

Now whether you've just decided to enter the daddy game for the first time or you've been putting in the time from day one, I can't promise you that there won't be bumps in the road with your children. Because at the end of the day, you can't make their choices for them. They will face temptations that you can't control; they will have decisions to make when you aren't watching. Sooner or later they will have to choose to follow the course you set for them and do the right thing. Or take the path of the rapper on television. Or the cool kid at school who cheats and doesn't mind being in the eighth grade at sixteen.

So this is not a call to perfection. Rather, it's a call to save our homes; and only by saving them can we save our communities, our cities, our states, and ultimately our country.

We've got to kill the Grinch.

You know him—the angry, abusive, always negative male who never smiles and thinks everything is a conspiracy. He's the neighborhood philosopher hanging out at the barbershop all day and sharing his reasons why O.J. didn't do it. His kids never see him having fun; they always see him mad, complaining about the job and why life is so bad. If you say it's a pretty day, he'll say, "Yeah, but it looks like rain; better stay inside." Negative! Negative! Negative!

We've got to kill the Grinch because the world sees us as grumpy, mean guys always telling the world, "You don't understand what I've gone through!" Brother, aren't you tired? Aren't you weary of always having to explain your dilemma? Not to deny the serious issues facing black men here in America; they are important challenges that must be met. But we can't wait until the battle is over before taking our positions as winners. Aren't you ready to take a deep breath, take stock of what you *do* have, and stop pointing out what you don't? I know I am.

We have to kill the Grinch because nobody forced us to skip class or stay in the locker room and not go to tutoring or sneak out to go drinking with our boys rather than take education seriously. We did things in our youth that contribute to the challenges we face now. We must take responsibility for that. It isn't your employer's fault that you didn't pay attention in class and just slid through, hanging out with your boy and 'nem. And now life is demanding something from you that you didn't prepare for. That our lives haven't gone the way we wanted them to doesn't justify taking it out on everybody around us. We can't stay angry at our wives who went to class and paid attention, because they can get better jobs than us. The only way to move forward from this bitterness is to admit our mistakes.

It's time to take the lemons and make lemonade. If no one else working at the bank has cornrows, you may want to cut yours off. Doing so *won't* mess with your blackness. You also may want to learn some way of communicating at your next job interview that doesn't involve ending every sentence with "y'know wha' I'm saying." And playing Nintendo with your son every day doesn't necessarily count as quality time, especially if he's eight years old and both of you are up way past his bedtime shooting people. Ask your son or daughter what they want to talk about. Find out what makes them happy. Read to them! Please! Ask them what a happy father looks like to them. You don't lose points for being honest; you lose points for not being there, mentally or physically. Lose the Grinch . . . and the corn-rows. (You're too old anyway!)

The influence and power black men have across a vast spectrum of American society, from the arts to sports—including the charisma of black leaders when they take the podium to speak to pivotal moments in the life of our society—are amazing. Nobody can deny the eloquence in Dr. King's voice when millions of colored people needed direction and leadership because they felt lost and needed hope. Who can forget the cleverness of the rhymes when Ali taunted an opponent? Or the pride we felt when the medical field recognized that they were blessed to have among them one of our best and brightest in Dr. Ben Carson? Remember how the stock prices for Nike soared when a black man had millions of kids—black, white, whatever—thinking they could "be like Mike" if they wore his shoes?

When we have spoken, the world has always listened. In technology, the black man has always made his mark. If we say this dance is *the* new dance, the world does it. If P. Diddy says kids will be wearing it on the streets this spring, it sells. We tell the world what's cool. We helped lead our armed forces to victory. We teach the new slang, the new flavor of the year. When seeking to influence or initiate change, from the bank to the block, we have proven time after time that we have a power both magnetic and infectious.

I spend a great deal of my life living in between the lines of color. For the last twenty years, my world has been filled with just as many white experiences as black ones. I just picked my kids up from a Christian youth camp they attend every summer where the percentage of kids of color is 2. But I was amazed at how the cheers, the song selections, and the terms were so obviously influenced by black men.

So with all the power black men wield, the cleverness of our style and the influence of our lives, why do we continue to allow the worst in us to be seen across television, radio, and newsstands on a weekly basis? Why can't the world see the strength of black men as we take a stand on what products are allowed into our communities? Or on what politicians say from our pulpits during the next election season? Or about what types of businesses are allowed on our corners?

We MUST have a high sense of honor and covering
for our most precious and sacred gift—the black woman.
She is the backbone of our community and the mother of our people. She has been, and will forever be, the glue that keeps our homes strong and our children healthy, both physically and spiritually. She is the heartbeat behind our voice and the key to our identity. Even when forced to carry dual roles with limited means, she has risen to the challenge to raise, nurture, and lead her home. She will forever be the epitome of the strength, hope, and beauty of the black experience.

But in my view no group in American culture degrades and exploits their women like black men degrade and exploit black women. Even though rock music in recent decades has seen hits like ZZ Top's "She's Got Legs," The Rolling Stones' "Honky Tonk Woman," and Warrant's "Cherry Pie," they sound like "Amazing Grace" next to the Ying Yang Twins' "Get Low," Uncle Luke's "Me So Horny" and Juvenile's classic "Back That Thang Up." We saw scantily dressed white women with bright red lipstick playing seductively in a Robert Palmer video, but the artist Nelly's sliding a credit card between the cheeks of an African-American woman's butt in his "Tip Drill" video serves as a public statement that we see our women as disposable and built for no other purpose but our personal gratification and satisfaction. And while some argue that women have a personal responsibility not to put themselves in those controversial positions, the black man—as protector and leader—has the responsibility to make wise, sober decisions on her behalf if she doesn't have a father or other male covering her life to do so. In short, the village and its leader should encourage her to make decisions that are responsible and self-respecting.

What have our women done to make us write songs so degrading to them? And then we encourage them to think of such songs as simple entertainment! But the lyrics aren't just words on the radio; they're a statement. A frame of mind. For whatever is in the heart, the mouth will speak. Do we not think of them as our mothers, our daughters, our sisters? Have we forgotten that they need us to build them up and protect them from a world that has undereducated them, underpaid them, and treated them like second-class citizens for generations? I ask you, brothers—what have they done to us? Are we paying them back for a lack of love we feel we received from our mothers? Are they paying for all the females in our lives who hurt us and left us feeling belittled and uncovered? If so, when is the debt fully paid? And how will they know?

Women have compromised themselves just to satisfy the seemingly insatiable urge of oversexed men. If they were treated with the respect they deserve, they wouldn't dress, dance, or give themselves to men in many of the ways they do.

I hate hearing women call themselves "bad b*tch" or "smart b*tch" because it gives power to a word that was meant to degrade and belittle. I also hate seeing black women in overplayed Hollywood roles as single parents with the baby daddy drama.

And the one that shakes my nerves most involves a young African-American woman driving down the street with her "man" laid back in the passenger seat, legs up on the dashboard, while he's being chauffeured around like a lazy king. Even if he just finished the night shift, that image portrays black men as weak and unable to lead. I realize that many will think my views judgmental, but these are serious times, times when the woman has had to go from supporting the partnership to leading it. The image we project not only to them but also to the world must be one of reclaiming our God-given responsibility as provider and source of her strength.

We are all aware that there are countries where women can't speak in public or where they must keep their faces covered in public, but ours is the country of Oprah, of the late Coretta, and of Michelle. Ours is *not* a country where women should feel that they must show their bodies to keep our interest. Or where they should have to wonder whether a man will be there for his children. And this definitely should not be a country where the love a woman feels from her man is abusive or conditional. Instead of turning to other women, our wives and daughters, mothers and sisters should first be able to turn to us.

We owe them an apology. Not for words' sake, but for life's sake. An apology expressed by our actions as well as our words, by a quest to make things right with our most sacred blessing. They need to see that neither hell nor high water will distract or destroy our commitment, that black men are collectively committed to protecting and caring not only for all women but especially for black women.

Whether you're a father who hasn't been there for your daughter or a playa with a history of multiple relationships with women, it's time to turn in the playa card, pimpin'; the time has come to end this ongoing generational curse stemming from how our fathers treated our mothers. We saw that curse lead men to have two and three relationships at a time in order to brag about their libido. But we are better than that. It's not too late to show the world the beauty of our women in the correct light—the light of education, leadership, wisdom, inner beauty, and pride. That's who they are. Not video hos, not jump-offs or booty calls, but our friends, our sisters, our matriarchs, our wives, our women. Our strong, black women.

Let's be the heart of the village.

Men holding each other accountable. Men being vulnerable, admitting our weaknesses to each other. Taking charge of the growing number of AIDS victims in our communities and among our women. No longer acting like all is well. Because all is not. We are broken, frustrated, hurting, and lost; we need a village with no hidden agendas. We don't need to be preached at—or to preach—from a higher podium; we need the answer to come down where the people are. We need to speak in love, not sound bites. We need to speak to the broken, to the poor, to those behind bars who've been lost in the judicial system. That's what Jesus would have done. Not the blue-eyed European Jesus painted by famous white artists, but the more geographically correct Middle Eastern bruised and physically ravaged Jesus, the one whose blood was red.

It may seem like I'm being incredibly hard on my brothers. But I do this out of overwhelming love for my people and a faith that black men have the skills, the gumption, and the strength to rise to the occasion. After all, we are a group that has surmounted unbelievable obstacles in the past to save our families and keep our communities together when the outside world only served us hatred and terror. After overcoming all of that, I know we are not going to succumb at a time when we have more opportunity than we have ever had before. This is not the time to give up, to walk away, to be weak or timid. I believe in our people. I believe in our men. I believe in our children. I still believe in our communities. And in leaders who are humble, transparent, and engaged for the long haul.

"So, Mr. Franklin, where do we go from here?"

I'm glad you asked.

Be a risk taker.

When I first started doing albums, it was all about going to a local radio station and playing your music for the station's program director. Everything I worked hard for seemed to hinge on his approval or disapproval. If he liked what he heard, he would put the song on the radio. My heart almost jumped out of my shirt when I drove down the street and my song was played for the first time. All because some guy I barely knew took a chance on a young musician with no name.

Black men, let's not keep playing the same song—about what didn't go right, about what "the man" did wrong, about how life is just unfair. Let's write a new melody. And give it new lyrics. A song that says, "What the enemy meant for bad, God meant for my good." Let's jump into the deep water and trust that, despite the preparation we *didn't* get for it, this is an opportunity and not a death sentence.

If you didn't get picked up by a professional team after college, that's okay. If the last relationship failed, then don't bring her into the next one. But take a chance on love. Not the TV show but the real thing. Don't do what's safe, do what's right— even if no one else is doing it. Don't be like those who end up on the sidelines. Or the guys who always want to talk about "back in the day." Be the one who takes a chance, who realizes that you are great at being you but horrible at being them. What God has for us will be greater than whatever we missed!

Truth can no longer be arbitrary.

After a few months in office, President Obama started making public service announcements encouraging men—for this chapter I'm saying *black* men—to stand up and be fathers to their children. I don't mean to continue hitting this horse, but it is the most powerful position in the world next to the mother's. When the president made that charge, no matter where you lived, you had to agree with his statement. If you were behind bars in San Quentin, in a law office in Chicago, at a travel agency in Houston, you had to agree that fathers need to man up to their responsibilities as dads. No one in his right mind viewed the statement as a mere opinion; it was a truth. That's how we need to start seeing the foundations of our villages, our families, our sexuality.

Self-respect needs to be the same thing in Colorado as it is in Cleveland. Character needs the same platform in Phoenix as it does in Philadelphia. If respecting your elders is truth, then everyone in the village needs to respond to it as such. All people, not just older people, need to feel the importance of that truth. If education is one of the most powerful things we can give our children, BET needs to express that truth. Entertainers need to express it. Sports figures need to express it. It can't be something instilled by just one household. The village needs to see it as a truth, and everyone needs to adjust to it. If not, our values and views will never be unified, and without unity, there is no power.

No more black passes.

You know the conversations we have behind closed doors; the things we discuss when it's just "us." And you know those things that continue to frustrate us privately but we don't address publicly. So we've got to deny the black pass—the pass that allows you to do whatever you want, live however you want, and say whatever you want just because you look like me. *But just because you look like me doesn't mean you're making me look better!* Those conversations we have about our black leaders, our black celebrities—whether they're in the local community or at the national level—well, if those leaders don't reflect the best of who we are, they can no longer get by because of their skin tone. I know black leadership is small, and we try to hold on to as many as we can, but we fail them if we don't love them. And to allow people to drive into a brick wall and kill themselves (and everyone else in the car) just because they were black leaves us with blood on our hands. No matter how much you love their music, their preaching, their speaking, their talent, or their skill, you owe it to the village to protect it from the poison of the lyrics and messages and lifestyles that don't promote a healthier village. And remember, being rich doesn't mean being healthy.

Let's not throw them away; let us remind them of the passion they had when they first started in public office, when they ran for city councilman. Let us show the young MC that his lyrics are like poetry when degrading statements about women are replaced with dignity and self-respect—and let's call the radio station and request those songs. Let us remind the young minister that it doesn't matter how many members you have on the roll; it's about touching just one soul.

We are a light shining on top of the mountain. We are a voice crying in the distance for justice. We are a song rewriting itself through every struggle in the key of hope. We are boys. We are men. Behind bars, behind bills, behind medicine, behind the mike, in politics, in the pulpit, we are soldiers!

Chapter Eight

THE BLUEPRINT FOR ADAM: MEN AND SEX

Sex. The word alone makes people uncomfortable. As soon as you read it, you may be overcome by pain, fear, anxiety, even anger. Isn't it amazing that just the mention of something God created as a beautiful expression of love between a husband and wife can conjure up so many different emotions? Something that allows God's creation to procreate, something that binds a man and woman's souls together, and joins them in a oneness that nothing else can, also makes us embarrassed and uncomfortable even to discuss. We get to share in God's character when, under his sovereign plan, the two become one. But some who read this chapter will have had experiences far removed from the bliss I've just described. Your experience may be filled with abuse, shame, and a feeling of being ill-equipped; so God's gift has never been experienced as He intended it to be, only as horror and shame.

In my experience, I find that many people, even church people, never had their parents talk to them thoroughly and honestly about sex. Some women tell me that their mothers and grandmothers taught them that sex was for making babies, not for pleasure. Some men have been taught by men other than their fathers, men whose lessons are laced not with love but lust. Some women tell me they think discussion of oral sex, pleasure, or anything that seems taboo is for fast women and women of the night, not for classy women and especially not for Christian women. One lady even tells me that when she was younger, she watched pornography not for pleasure but to learn what her parents never taught her.

As kids, most of us never had Bible sermons from the youth pastor explaining God's plan for sex. We were just told, "Don't do it! God says wait until you're married!" Right. But what about being young, with hormones on crack, and curious about these feelings and emotions that arise every time I go to P.E. and little Susie is doing the splits? What do I do with that? Help me, preacher!

I've told the story before, but just in case you haven't heard it, I'll tell it again. I remember after I gave my heart to Christ at fifteen going to my pastor. I started having sex or sexual experiences when I was nine, so by the time I came to Christ the damage had already started. I went to the pastor and expressed my struggle of trying to live out my new spiritual commitment; I needed help and advice on what to do with desires that didn't go away when I said "yes" to Jesus.

He sat back in his chair, thinking for a moment, and then took a puff of his cigar. "Aw boy, you're young, you'll grow out of it," he said. That was it? That was the advice I'd been waiting for all my young, horny life? Yeah! Thanks, pastor! Thanks. For . . . nothing.

So we struggle with sex. We desire sex. We are confused by sex. Some of us were touched in wrong ways; some of us played little neighborhood games involving sex and learned the wrong lessons. Some of us were even abused by bad interpretations of what the Bible says; or maybe it wasn't even what the Bible says, but just someone's opinion of what the Bible says. So we were abused by a bad interpretation of a misunderstanding of what the Bible says! We had mothers who didn't teach us; daddies who molested us; boyfriends, girlfriends, husbands, or wives who added to the pain of our promiscuity. So that beautiful song, sex, was often sung wrongly.

Many churches even approach homosexuality in the wrong way. We've preached from a homophobic bent. We take the man who cheats on his wife or the organist who goes through the women in the choir like a drawer of socks and we slap them on the wrist. But we humiliate the person struggling with desire for the same sex. That has been not only wrong, but also downright unchristian. We are more compassionate about struggles we understand. Although we can never compromise what the Bible says about homosexuality, it's very important to bring a measure of love and caring to anyone engaged in that lifestyle. And if we aren't willing to walk through life's issues with people, but rather choose to stand on the sideline and judge, we need to be quiet and take a careful look at our own Christianity.

Sex is here. It is a gift from God. And done God's way, it allows us, His creation, to participate in His likeness. But if we continue being super-spiritual about it, if we continue to be ashamed even to talk about it, relationships will continue to suffer. And people will continue to die. So are you ready? In the interest of trying to turn around all the bad lessons that many men out there have been taught about sex and of forming a blueprint for a healthy male sexual life, let's talk about sex, baby!

Men love sex.

I don't care how you break it down, how you express it—men *love* sex. Understanding that our past experiences affect and shape our mental programming and interpretation of sex, I will limit myself to the thousands of men I've met speaking at conferences, schools, and youth seminars as well as my history and that of my local homeboys at the neighborhood barbershop. And here's the upshot: *Men love sex!* Period. Exclamation mark!

Yes, we can be just as complex and moody as our sisters. And we don't always do a good job of expressing what we want. So here's what we *do* want—a best friend, a road dawg, a homie, a lover, a soldier, a woman who plays pool and gets mad when her favorite team loses. We want romance. And we also want a little freak in our woman (for those who aren't comfortable with this level of detail, I'll leave it there). Please don't mistake the fact that men—and this includes all of us, even the one who dresses in Dockers and didn't get the e-mail about Puff Daddy changing his name to Diddy—love sex.

We can act like we want our women to be our mamas; we can whine, complain, and sometimes make them feel like single parents, but we love sex. We love the texture of a woman's skin. The softness of her voice in our ear. The flow of her legs when she walks into the bedroom. Her laughter when we jump out of the bathroom wearing drawers that are too tight but make us feel like The Rock. The sway in her back that leads down to the top of her bottom. The boldness inside her that, in the middle of lovemaking, allows her to stop, grab our face, look us dead in the eyes and tell us "it's yours."

Even those of us in the faith, whether Holy Ghost–filled Pentecostals or conservative Evangelicals—when we marry the love of our lives, we don't want to lose that fire when the lights turn off (or even when they stay on, because most men like to watch!). We love our wives to pray for us, go to church with us, and bless God for their families. But there is a different type of hand laying that a husband wants to continue when we turn off Shirley Caesar and put on some Maxwell. We need a passionate, freaky, playful, spontaneous, romantic wife, who loves being with us as much as we love being with her. A wife who cooks eggs in an apron with her Manolos on and won't mind sneaking in her mama and daddy's powder room between seconds at Thanksgiving.

Men want that; men *need* that. It's our love language, our way of feeling "big" and valuable. And just in case you think this is limited to men with a certain cultural background or a history like mine, let's look at some men who've never lived in the hood, men who had fathers and never experienced the baby mama drama.

Can we begin with all the politicians over the last twenty years who've posed perfectly with their Ivy League sweethearts only to be destroyed by headline news clippings of affairs and prostitution rings? Men whose wives smile and stand by them, sometimes knowing that, when they were alone with their husbands, something just didn't feel right. But instead of being bold and confronting that gut feeling, they held on to the reputation, the perks, the amenities, and hid for another day.

Can we talk about the pastors and religious leaders who've stumbled? Some have—or *had*—beautiful wives, women you'd never think would become victims of infidelity. Despite being used by God powerfully to affect millions of lives, these men fell—hurting not only the women and children who stood with them and sacrificed so much, but also a heavenly Father who once again takes it on the chin in society's eyes. Yet another stone is thrown at the church and the faith is dishonored once more.

Now, please don't misunderstand my motives. I am not attempting to bash religious leaders who are good men with good motives. How can I? But by the grace of God there go I. Rather, I'm speaking of men in general—whether they stand on the steps of the church or walk the halls of Congress, whether they pass legislation or the plate. Men love sex.

I asked a group of men in church once how many of them

had sexual thoughts through most of the day. When the hands went up, it looked like somebody was giving away tickets to the Super Bowl. I know that some men and most women won't agree with these observations, but they're true. Recently, I asked an older friend of mine, who happens to be a prominent pastor, "When does this mental struggle end for a man?" He smiled. "Son," he said, "I can tell you it ain't sixty-one!"

Now I know some women are saying, "Kirk, I did *everything* my man wanted me to do! When my husband wanted a freak, I was his freak. When he flew back into town and wanted me to take off the rollers and put on something cute, I did it. But he *still* cheated. He *still* hurt me. I did everything he wanted; even when it wasn't me, even when I felt like somebody else was in the bed, I still was there. And he *still* cheated. Why?"

We sanctified the sickness.

Once I was in Africa with a group of guys on a long musical tour. We were gone from our homes for several weeks. As the trip was coming to an end, some of the fellas in the group—me included— were out eating and laughing. Someone at the table said, "Man, when I get home, my wife better get ready! I've been gone for weeks and it's going to be nothing nice!"

After that, every brother at the table began talking about how *his* wife needed to take the kids over to Nana's and do some calisthenics because big papa is coming home! And trust me, I'm giving you the Sunday morning version of the conversation.

Sitting there listening, it just dropped inside of me, "Man, we sound like we did when we were young, going out on a Saturday night trying to holla at some females, when our agenda was not to have a relationship but to get it on and popping and get our freak on." We didn't sound any different as we sat there talking about our wives, our "church."

Timid about taking the risk of being the punk at the table, I went where no man has gone before. "Fellas," I asked, "what do y'all think would happen if, when we flew home, the first thing we did was take the kids, schedule a spa appointment, tell her to take the day for herself, and then when she came back, we gave her a few hours of adult conversation, rubbed her feet, ran some bathwater, fixed her some Kool-Aid, and then let the chips fall where they may? If y'all fall asleep, you fall asleep. If you make the earth move that night, call the paramedics. But let it be love, not an erection, that sets the course."

Silence.

Then one guy said with hesitance, "You know, that would take the pressure off a brother to have to perform."

Another cat said, "Man, you're right."

Then the conversation moved from *Showtime at the Apollo* to the question, "Why do men do that to themselves?" Why do we create the pressure of feeling that we always need to perform in bed to make our women feel that we are good? Believe it or not, some of us guys feel the need to perform because we've been doing it all our lives.

Here's the deal.

Most men have had sexual experiences before they got married. And what those experiences were determines how deeply they've affected him. It could be one girl; it could be twenty. (Believe me, I'm understating this!) Whatever his experiences— strip clubs, prostitutes, one-night stands, *whatever*—he learned sex in a performance-oriented way. Because we all know that when you're single, it's all about who's going to outdo whom. So the male body and mind are introduced to all kinds of things called "love" that are really something else. Whatever those things are, they certainly *aren't* love as God intended it to be, and they don't create the intimacy that He planned for a husband and wife.

So a man gets tired of living that way; he gets tired of bachelor parties, booty calls, getting his freak on, one-night stands.
And he decides to settle down, to get married. He wants to stop
"loving" women the wrong way, so he decides to find a nice girl
to ask to be his wife, his best friend for life. He says to himself,
"Instead of doing all of these things with women all over the city
(or globe!), I'm going to stop living wrong, settle down, and
just be with one girl."

But here's the problem: If he never goes through the process
of "divorcing" his past, having accountability and a spiritual
walk that digs *deep* into the issues that each of them brings to
the table and the realization that one woman can't do what ten
can do, then after a few months or years or babies or weight
gain or hair loss, he will realize—"they" will realize—that the
only thing he did was take a single man and put a ring on his
finger. He "sanctified" his sickness. Marriage never really addressed his real issue, the underlying one, because he never
bothered to renew his mind, to stop letting his past experiences
determine his outlook.

And if his environment and homeboys didn't change, they
just reinforced his sickness. Brothers, please take what I'm saying
seriously! Some of you have experienced the kind of thing I'm
talking about when you went back to your ten- or twenty-year
high school reunion and ran into your old flame or your old
crush. *(Everybody who had a curl and rocked the high-top Reeboks
with the Velcro, make some noise!)* Remember how your mind
started to race as y'all began to reminisce about "back in the
day"? And remember that uncomfortable, guilty feeling when
the conversation crossed the line and y'all talked about that night
in the car after prom?

Ouch!

Even though you are happily married with children, a great career and all that . . . and everything in your life has changed . . . everything, that is, except for that soul tie. And if you aren't careful, that conversation will go into water so deep it will drown you. And destroy everything you've worked so hard to build. I've talked to so many people who've had this experience and can't believe that, after all those years and all these new pounds, they could still find themselves getting sweaty palms over the captain of the football team. Or feel their hearts beat faster while driving there, hoping to see Miss Congeniality of the class of '88!

Soul ties. The thing that can make you hear an old-school slow jam and think of somebody you haven't seen in years. Soul ties. The thing that makes old people who've been together for years finish each other's sentences. Don't you wish mama had told you when you were young that, when you lie with someone, you lie not just with her body but also with her soul? And whatever condition the other person's soul is in, you are guaranteed to take a piece with you—whether you want to or not. Instead of being amazed at her booty, you should have focused on her mind. Don't you wish somebody had told you that sex as a single is like a contest, that it's about who turns out whom? The man performs for the night and maybe a follow-up session or two, but the woman plays for keeps.

This is so important because men don't realize that they *do* have wives who want to please them, who really do *want* to make their men happy. Most women with common sense (and women, please don't let me down here!) don't marry men they are not sexually attracted to. I don't care how deep spiritually you are, normally you don't marry somebody who doesn't light your fire. So when a woman doesn't feel turned on by her man, and doesn't want to please him in the bedroom, something has gotten disconnected. If a woman begins to feel dirty, to feel that it's always "lights, camera, action," to feel that the relationship's focal point is sexual performance, she shuts down. If she doesn't feel special to her man, if she doesn't feel that, even though she still has some of the baby weight from having *his* kids, he will still drink her bathwater, she *won't* be all he wants her to be; and he'll think it's her, but actually it's *his* sickness showing itself.

Please hear my heart when I make this observation. I believe that premarital counseling can be a joke. Understand, it's not meant to be a joke. But if it isn't real, transparent, and ugly, it doesn't get to the core of what people really bring into their relationships, especially in the area of sex. Most people enter into premarital counseling all aglow, grinning from cheek to cheek. They have their plans, the cake is picked, the guest list has gone out, and they are happier than a chubby kid on his way to Krispy Kreme.

So they enter the counselor's office with plans to be husband and wife. The counselor explains that God honors marriage; with big smiles, they say, "Yes!"

Then the counselor points out that they will have rough days; when those days come, they'll need to hang in there. And they say, "Yes!"

"Don't forget," the counselor continues, "communication is the key, so don't stop talking." And they say, "Yes!"

And so the session continues in this fashion, with this generic almost antiseptic approach to truth, an approach that seems more like Sunday school than reality. If they leave the counselor's office with this neat, clean, all-too-pretty perspective on life together, they leave with only half the truth. Because every marriage—every relationship, for that matter—has its share of bumps and bruises, ups and downs, they need to have a skanky, gritty, butt-naked conversation about what life's like when the show is over. And believe me, *every* show comes to an end!

If I were the counselor, the session would go like this.

"Are you both virgins?"

If the answer is "yes," I ask whether they've had *any* sexual experiences, either with each other or with others. Because these days the definition of "virginity" allows even virgins to have a background filled with sexual experiences that are loaded guns, even if the bullets are smaller caliber.

If the answer is "no," then I continue: "Have you had intercourse or some type of experimentation with each other?"

Suppose they say "yes."

I ask the young lady, "Is there something he likes you to do sexually?"

"Yes."

"Do you enjoy doing the thing he likes you to do?"

"Not really, but I do it because he likes it."

Then I ask the young man, "Do you understand that there is something you like sexually that she doesn't enjoy, that she only does because you like it? Do you understand what that means— that after a few years and a couple of babies, she may not find that appealing? Can you live with that?"

The point is that we have to be realistic about sex and marriage; otherwise, issues will come up that catch us off guard.

Eleven years ago, Tammy and I ran into a bump in our relationship. I first noticed it after our first child was born; she seemed disconnected sexually and it felt like the fire was burning out in the bedroom. When she wanted a second child, I was hesitant because the lovemaking wasn't right. She promised that I would remain a priority and that loving me would be at the top of her list. After the birth of our second child, though I could see her trying to keep her end of the agreement, the disconnectedness slowly started to come back. Having always felt rejected by the women in my life, I came to believe that Tammy had fallen out of love with me.

When we went together for counseling, I was prepared to make a great presentation on all the good I was doing in the relationship—providing for Tammy and the children; coming home every night to be with her and only her; flowers, dates, trips, expensive gifts, all the things that TV says make a woman happy. I just knew the counselor would look at my wife and say, "Girl, you've lost your mind!" But when Tammy began to express herself, her words left me speechless.

You see, my promiscuous past haunted my present performance. From childhood, I had been given to unhealthy sexual experiences with girls. That, combined with watching "adult" material as a little boy, created in me an unrealistic vision of what sex is supposed to be. And even though I'd admitted all this to Tammy during our second year of marriage, that admission didn't erase all the thoughts, appetites, and expectations that my experiences had given me. I didn't know that I'd made my wife feel cheap, dirty, and unloved. I was taking the advice I'd received as a kid from men in the hood about what women like and how to please them in the bedroom. But I'd never asked my wife what she liked, what made her feel sexy, or most important, what made her feel loved. And as for making her feel loved, the minks couldn't do it. Neither could the surprise trips to the islands. As men, we think those things should, but they can't. Tammy had shut down; and until that day in counseling, I had no idea why.

Men try to blend the single man together with the married one. But that leads to self-destruction. Look at our attitudes even about bachelor parties. We convince ourselves that this is the safe way to have one more crazy night with the boys and some females before we stand in front of God and witnesses to ask for His blessings. So even the night before we make our vows and become husbands, we keep adding to the sickness. And from the wedding night on, we expect our wives to meet expectations that are simply unrealistic.

Most men don't even realize how deep this goes. Most of us don't set out to hurt and manipulate the women in our lives. We do what we've seen; we follow the pattern we saw our dads follow, some of them even with our own mothers. And having "quick sex" has kept us from tapping in to the emotional or vulnerable space in our hearts.

The bump in our marriage helped me realize how much I didn't know, how lost I was (and sometimes still am) when it comes to connecting with my wife on a deep, intimate level. Until then, I was performing. But now the show is over. Once life has kicked in—after you've buried a couple of friends and seen your career and children change—you lie with your wife differently; sometimes you just hang on to her for dear life.

Most of us men can't risk being that vulnerable with our wives; we fear they'll see that we are really *not* good lovers. That's why our wives sometimes get the "bam bam" approach in the bedroom. That may be fine for quickies. But when they need us to go to a deeper level—one of mutual openness and weakness—we have no idea what they're talking about. So we avoid our wives, turning to the Internet or finding someone (or even some-*thing*) that doesn't demand that we be emotional Clark Kents. Hmm . . . that may not be a good example because even Superman had to deal with his kryptonite, and King David had his Beyoncé—sorry Bathsheba!

And for many, the show is coming to an end. But when that happens to a man without his understanding why, he develops a hidden anger toward his wife because who she was in bed is not who she is now.

I firmly believe that God has designed sexual intimacy according to certain specifications. I promise not to get preachy, but fellas please just give your boy a second. Some marriages have been totally shattered because the husbands brought to the bedroom experiences that a healthy, functional marriage wasn't meant to handle. If you've had multiple partners, lap dances at strip bars, women who were there only for the purpose of sexual pleasure, and hour after hour on the Internet, how in the world can a mom with two kids and a full-time job meet your unrealistic expectations or live up to your unhealthy programming? She can't. We can't create a culture of free love, sex as a stress reliever or a man's prerogative, and a "do what feels good" mentality without repercussions.

But in the midst of the hopelessness that some of you might be feeling, it is *not* too late to get it right. I enjoy sneaking in on my son when he's playing a new video game. He gets so frustrated when he starts to lose because he hates not winning. Instead of hanging in there and learning from his mistakes, he'll turn off the game so it will erase his score; then he can start fresh. Unfortunately, life doesn't work quite like that, but it's never too late to make a fresh start. In time, your old score can be erased and, through God's grace and new habits, your love life can have a new beginning. But I would advise you not to be like my eight-year-old; learn from your mistakes, because every lesson not learned will be repeated.

Trust me, no one was more messed up than your boy. By God's grace, I'm better; and I'm *still* learning. In the interest of helping men construct a blueprint for sex that is strong and healthy, I offer here some of the things I've learned in forming my own blueprint.

Let it marinate.

Sounds funny, doesn't it? What I mean is this: Men think about sex almost all the time. Some experts say that sexual thoughts run through a man's mind every fifteen minutes or so. So every time our wives offer us a little affection, we try to turn it into sex. Our wives become reluctant to show us any affection because they fear that we won't simply take it as a loving touch, a caring hug, or an "I love you" kiss. As soon as most of us get a little touch, it's "Girl, you've gone and started something! Lock the door!" That'll frustrate a woman. Her need to be loved her way never gets met, and there's no passion when you finally do get into the bedroom.

So try spending an extended period of time talking about what *she* wants to talk about. (I say *extended* because my brothers need to know that it must be more than just during commercials.) Laugh at some silly television shows she likes; give her a long, soft, passionate kiss; and then go *back* to watching the show. (Women, you like?) Rub her feet. Ask her what she has going on next week and how you can help with the kids to take some stress off her. Finally, when it's time for bed, read her one of her favorite books, rub her hair. If she has a weave, rub her temples. And tell her that you thank God for her, that your life would be jacked up if you hadn't been given such a priceless gift. And then go to sleep.

You still there, brothers? Don't turn the page yet; trust me on this one. You need to make deposits and then just let the love-making marinate. Don't let your erection run the show. The difference between grandmama's cooking and yours is that granny started cooking Sunday's dinner on Saturday night. Even while she was at church, she had the oven set on low; things were marinating. When you sat at her table after church, you were enjoying what had been prepared the day before. Your cooking is instant and microwavable. That's why it's cold when you cut into it. And so is she!

Now she may not believe you at first because you've lived like a sex-starved dog. But after a season of communicating to her that you don't want sex to be the focal point of your marriage, she may start to feel that she can trust this new man, whoever he is. And, brother, when she does, the fire you've been trying for so long to light will have a brilliance that you haven't seen in years. I wouldn't sell it if I hadn't bought it. I'm not only a client, I'm the love president.

Ask her what she likes.

Men, you have to be ready for her answer. But wouldn't you rather she be who she is rather than someone she deep-down detests? Because if she detests who she has to be for you, she'll also detest you. If she doesn't like certain positions, or if certain things make her feel dirty or unloved, find out what she *does* like, what makes *her* happy, what turns *her* on.

Here's a tip: Don't ask during sex. You may think it's sexy to ask in the moment, "Whatcha like, baby?" But you need to remember that certain things you did when you were single may not work in a "real life" relationship. Find a time away from the act to ask her—playfully and nonconfrontationally—what makes her happy in bed. And when you get your answer, don't keep asking! Don't make it a mountain she always has to climb. Because if you do, she won't talk. And, even though it's not real, the show will continue.

Men, we can be very selfish in bed. We can make our women feel that, if they aren't fulfilling every desire we have, they're pushing us to be satisfied somewhere else. Remember, brothers, our women can't make us do anything that we don't choose to do ourselves. The divine blueprint, God's Word, reminds us that each man is pulled away by his own lustful desires. We must remember that we aren't in bed by ourselves. And if what she likes doesn't always lead to the main meal, learn how to enjoy the appetizers. (I know—that borders on corny!)

Your goal shouldn't be just to release, but to become one with your best friend, your lover, your wife. Now, if she wants to bring the freak mama out and make your toes curl, praise the

Lord. Ain't nothing wrong with a woman pleasing her man and fulfilling his desires, but she needs to know that she doesn't have to live up to your past experiences; that you love her *for her*, for who she *really* is.

According to women I've talked to, men can get most of what they want if their women feel safe. *Safe!* What does that mean? Does it mean they're afraid we'll try something that might throw their backs out? No. By "safe," they mean that, before they get to the bedroom, they *know* there is no other person you'd rather be with, that the lights will be on when y'all come home from church, that she can drive the car without having to hide it at her mama's house to keep the repo man at bay, that hell will freeze over before you let harm come to her or the kids. She needs to be able to say, "He's got me." *Safe.*

During our second year of marriage, I did something for our anniversary that I thought would earn me lots of player points. We were in the presidential suite of a five-star hotel in Beverly Hills. I had a private chef cook dinner for us in the suite and surprised her with a fur and a big, big ring. Then I sat her on top of the piano and played her favorite songs for her. (Player! Player!) Thinking I had prepared a great environment for intimacy, I proceeded.

But no matter how good my performance, I couldn't help noticing that she was disconnected. My best performance didn't address her deepest needs. Outside the bedroom, I hadn't made her feel safe. Instead, my old performance actually led her to shut down. My past experiences led her to feel unsafe, and so she didn't feel free to give herself to me completely. I hadn't seen it earlier because the "show" hadn't gotten to the "intermission" yet.

After much pain and growth, I've learned to speak her love language. She loves to watch me help with the kids. She loves for me to help around the house. It turns her on when I choose to lose arguments. I've discovered what she likes.

So find out what *she* likes. Remember, you no longer exist for yourself; you exist for each other. I wish I'd known that before I bought that ring and coat!

Ask God to heal your sexuality.

This is where I need to bring God into our discussion of sex. Sex is His gift to us. So when we make the gift more of a curse than a blessing, we need to go back to the manufacturer.

Since He created it, only He can fix it. But the question remains: Once the truth about sex is revealed, how will you respond to it? Will you respond like the men in your life who think it's okay to have a little something—a little some*one*—on the side, men who think it's our nature to be driven by sex all the time? Or will you see your marriage, your family, and you yourself as too precious to be destroyed because what's inside your pants can be controlled? The generational curse can end with you.

When my wife and I started having trouble in our sex life, I'd been free from pornography for about two years. And when it got bad for us, I knew I couldn't go back to my old lifestyle because that would only make things worse. So I felt hurt and lost. Since I wanted to be faithful to her in the midst of what we were going through, I had only one option—to pray. So I simply prayed, "Father, heal me sexually; sanctify my sexuality." I don't know how I came to those words; I don't even know whether I understood what I was asking. But I was desperate and things were *not* good in bed at home.

The first thing I realized was that help would not come until I realized I needed it. It doesn't matter how good a doctor is, how skilled in his profession he is, how experienced in making diagnoses he is—if you don't think you're sick enough to need his help, he can't help you. And even if you muster up enough strength to visit him, his first question will be, "Tell me where it hurts." So you have a part to play in getting help for your problem. The doctor must know the exact problem before he can treat you. In acknowledging that I had a problem, I was preparing myself to hear the diagnosis and receive the solution.

When you acknowledge your problem to God, you're saying, *Father, I am weak. I am helpless. I haven't been making love your way; I was never taught to do it your way. Help me because I can't help myself. I can't fix me. I need you to do what I can't.*

I'm not trying to bore you or push you to be a weird, super-saint dude. I'm simply suggesting that everything else you've tried has failed to fix the deepest problem. Vacations, spicing up your love life, whatever else you've tried to solve the problem has only amounted to putting a Band-Aid on a cancer. You need a specialist, a chief surgeon, someone who knows where you are and where you need to be.

When you leave the doctor's office, you have a diagnosis. You're sick. Your past experience, the things your father didn't teach you, the bad Bible teaching you've heard about sex, and all the locker-room conversations have programmed you to fail. But the doctor has a prescription for you. And that prescription involves a process.

I think one of the most amazing things about the fruits of the spirit that the Bible talks about is the gift of self-control. Surely this is something most men can relate to, because it is the monster that we struggle with in so many areas of our lives, from the time we're young boys until well into our old age. Self-control is what protects our relationships, our careers, our children, our lifestyles. Without it, we will succumb to the flesh every time, whether that flesh is in the guise of the new girl with the big booty asking if you're busy after work, or the cop who has pulled you over and thrown a few nasty insults in your face in the process of writing your ticket, or the boss who sees fit to disrespect you in front of the entire staff. Without it, you will face many regrets as you find yourself staring mournfully at the ceiling in that new girl's bed, or being thrown into the backseat of that cop's cruiser in handcuffs, or trudging out of that office carrying a cardboard box containing the framed pictures of your kids that you now have to find another way to support because you cursed out your supervisor. I think it's dope that God showed us that something like self-control is the fruit of the spirit. You would expect that love, peace, and those things connected to our emotions would be the fruit, but he threw self-control in the basket, and that changes the game. Just because you see it and desire it doesn't mean it's for you. Even with our jobs. We got people thinking that more means more blessed. But in the process of getting that bigger job, you're away from your family more and your marriage isn't sizzling anymore. You got the clothes, you got the junk, but you don't have the home anymore. So men need to ask the Lord to help us with our self-control, to be humble enough to accept that we ain't strong enough to withstand the flesh by ourselves. We need His help. He can fix it.

Don't feed the animals.

You've lived a long time with the old man that you were—with your old habits and tricks, and *they* don't die easily. We didn't learn in marriage class that, when two become one, you bring your old past with you. And that old past makes you expect a certain diet. But you must not feed *old* food to the *new* man. Animals in the zoo shouldn't be given the food you brought in your lunchbox. They are on a strict diet prepared for them by the zoo's nutritionist, and anything else will hurt them. However much the gorilla likes your ham-and-bacon sandwich, if it isn't on his diet, what tastes good at the moment will harm him later. And your main concern at the zoo should be the animals' welfare.

Now rather than focusing on yourself and whatever tastes good at the moment, you should love God and your spouse enough to commit yourself, no matter how good the old diet tasted or how much you liked it, to not feed the new man what the old man ate. Having little nasty jokes that you share with your single brothers may be funny at the time, but it keeps you vulnerable to those old thoughts and habits. You need instead to learn to hate what God hates and to love what God loves.

"But Kirk," you say, "you're not being realistic! It ain't that easy; old habits are *hard* to break!"

Hard, yes; impossible, no. Not, at least, if you remember what's at stake.

If you learned that a Civil War–era treasure chest containing at least $20 million in gold and jewels was buried fifty feet deep in your backyard, I doubt that your full-time job, the front row tickets to your favorite team's game, or anything else—whether good or bad—would keep you from digging and sweating late into the night to find that "buried treasure." (I'm going somewhere with this, so please stay with me!) You might get tired and frustrated because your tools keep breaking or rainstorms slow you down, but you wouldn't quit, you wouldn't stop. You know that what lies beneath is worth the hard work, the calluses on your hands, the sacrifice of free time. You know the value of the reward will be much greater than the value of your labor.

Ask God to show you the value of your marriage, the value of connecting with your wife on a deep level. Instead of looking elsewhere for pleasure, you need to seek the "hidden treasure" in your own backyard. If you do, you'll gain from no longer having those "guy" conversations with your boys at the office about the new girl who has a body like Beyoncé (why does she keep coming up?) and from realizing that the girl on the Internet site is somebody's daughter, as well as God's creation. For while it hurts others as well, continuing to eat the old food when you are a new creation hurts you most of all.

If you're weak and can't get there by yourself, tell your boys what you're trying to do, that you're embarking on a "personal invasion." Ask your boys to help you become the new man you were created to be. And if they are the kind of dudes who don't care about that "right living" stuff . . . it might be time to let them go. So don't be surprised if—while you're going through this process, this "detox" from the junk that's been inside you—you start to lose some friends and the journey involves some loneliness.

Once when training for a video shoot, my trainer put me on a strict diet. I remember going out to eat one night with my wife and some friends. They ordered ribs, catfish, collard greens, pork chops, and every other ungodly part of a pig you can imagine; I had a grilled chicken salad with orange and apple slices, half a baked potato, and water. Hmm . . . I must admit that I thought some unchristian words that day because everybody else had whatever they wanted while I ate only what was necessary for reaching my goal for the video. I felt like an outsider at the table (and probably should have stayed home) because trying to hang out with people whose diet was not like mine frustrated me and made the night uncomfortable.

While you are adjusting to a new diet, it might be hard for you to hang out with people eating what you know is no longer good for you. You may have to eat, and sometimes live, by yourself. That can be lonely. And it can leave you feeling isolated. But God sometimes requires you to make drastic moves to protect His investment in *you*.

In your home, the dishes you use every day are easier to reach than the ones you use only on special occasions. The ones for special occasions are put up high, away from the kids and guests. They are on reserve because they serve a special purpose. Stop treating your sex life like a Dixie cup; it's special and needs to be put up high on reserve.

Imagine all the times Jordan stayed after practice. Or all Michael Jackson's late-night rehearsals while working on the *Thriller* album. Or all the frat parties Dr. King passed on to study for finals. Before greatness becomes public, it must be born in private.

That's the way it is for you, too. *Your greatest moments as a married man come from who you are in private.* How you manage your thought life. How you value your wife. How you fill your life with love rather than lust. How you never see yourself as affair-proof, because no matter how spiritual you are, it can happen to you. And how you depend on the gift's Giver, Christ Himself.

Most men fall because they don't spend time with "the manufacturer," they don't read the manual, they have no personal accountability, they put no boundaries on their friendships with women, and they don't think it can happen to them.

Stay weak. Don't be prideful. Go to "the doctor" for daily checkups. Don't feed the animal. Remember your new diet. Change your friends if necessary. It doesn't matter how long you've known them; if they're not eating what you're eating, they can't help you. Finally, work to find your buried treasure. And ask yourself how bad do you want it.

This is the blueprint for a great and healthy sexual relationship with your spouse. And a very important part of the new you that's being built. A blueprint for being complete in your marriage, because everything you do comes from a healed place. Now when you get your freak on, it's love-centered, not self-centered; when you think about your wife sexually, you think of your queen, not your jump-off (or booty call). You'll be happy when it's fireworks, and you'll be happy when it's a drizzle. Because the two of you are more than the sum parts of your sex.

Of course, men will still think about sex too much . . . and I bet Beyoncé is a very nice person!

Chapter Nine

THE BLUEPRINT FOR EVE: WOMEN AND SEX

Your turn, ladies!

Women, I am in awe of you! I am your biggest fan. Nothing to me is more powerful and inspiring than the atmospheric change created when a woman walks into a room. I watch you. You love to feel pretty. Even sexy. To hope that someone finds you attractive, smart, beautiful. Doesn't matter if you're full-figured or a middle-aged, divorced mother of two. I guarantee you there's a guy somewhere, maybe right under your nose, who finds you to be the most beautiful creature in the world. As you read this, the short little manager with the earring who speaks to you every time you go to Target is just dying to make a move!

We all watch you, women. How you walk when you think you have on something cute. How you dress as soon as you lose the weight from the baby. How you speak with your eyes when you think a guy is fine. How you accent the parts of your body that you think are attractive. We watch you. Most of you understand what society finds appealing, attractive, *sexy*. Billions—yes, *billions*—of dollars are spent on treatments, hair extensions, lipstick, makeup, implants—all because you hear, read, and watch what the world calls "sexy."

You talk about each other. You compliment one another. You are catty to the woman who kills the room she just walked into better than you. You point out your friends' attractive qualities; you dwell on things about yourself that make you feel unattractive.

We watch you. We may not always understand you; we may *never* understand you. But we watch you. When it comes to your appearance, you're meticulous. When you feel inspired, your conversations can be deep and insightful. *Surprise, ladies! We do like intelligent women!* We love that you laugh at our jokes, that you seem interested in the lives we lead, that your eyes brighten when we talk about our dreams, and that you aren't afraid to let a spark be seen even if you've made a commitment not to light it until you're married.

But (you knew the "but" was coming, right?) my beautiful, intelligent, strong women, you're not always honest. It may not be intentional, but still you can be deceptive. For the truth is, you are sometimes so busy trying to win that the real you isn't even the one at the race, or at dinner or the movie. And if something sexual happens before marriage, the real you isn't necessarily the one in the bedroom.

When a woman performs, it's even more distorted than when a man does. God designed your soul for commitment, for forever relationships. But if your mother, older sister, or friend had bad relationships or experiences, they can mess up the purest heart and leave the men in your lives angry, lost, and confused. Some women were taught "this is how you get a man, and this is what you do to keep a man." Women who've been through distorted sexual experiences can be just as manipulative as men. And this can lead to the "car crash syndrome" when you do get into a serious relationship. Let me be more explicit.

If a man's presentation to a woman his first time meeting her is heavy on the sexual side—with sexy little statements and an obvious agenda for the night ahead—a healthy-minded woman will end the date feeling disrespected and uncomfortable; mind you, I said a *healthy* woman. But if a woman's first date with a man is heavy on the low-cut dress, showing the "twins," the eyelashes bouncing up and down, the little innuendos and flirtatious mannerisms, it may lead to the bedroom. And after that, if there is good conversation and a deeper connection the next morning, a relationship *could* develop.

Now, like the man, this programs the woman. Regardless of what she has previously learned from her environment, or from society, or even from religion, she now "learns" that sex is the way to create a relationship, that relationships are *based* on sex. And she learns this lesson well. Even if she has been raised to believe that "ladies don't talk about *it*" or "'nice girls' don't do *that*," she comes to believe that relationships can be built on sex—when in fact good, healthy sex is built on the foundation of a good, committed relationship. So in the beginning, if the woman is not careful, the man will take her for what she says she is and what she indicates she'll do. He will expect her to always perform the way she did initially. And their relationship will be based on her meeting his expectations sexually—regardless of how unrealistic they are. So when a woman uses sex or her sexuality as the driving force when first getting to know a man, she is setting herself, and him, on a road to destruction.

Please understand that my thinking grows out of my research, out of my own experiences. Of all my male friends, I have always been the most metrosexual. I was raised by a woman; I spent most of my life primarily around women. Even as a young man, I had sexual experiences with women much older than me. There was always pillow talk, neighborhood talk, lots of listening.

And I know how guys feel when the ugly thug with dope

money gets the pretty girl who won't give them the time of day because they play the piano at church. I know how contradictory a woman seems when she says she wants a good man, but then if he doesn't look like Denzel or Brad Pitt that good man can't even get her phone number. Possibly not even her e-mail address.

Some of you want a man to respect you, but your jeans fit to show your thong when you bend over to tie "little man's" shoes. Or your butterfly tattoo peeks out when you kneel down at the altar on Sundays. We men don't understand how some of you can be so Christian and yet so materialistic at the same time. And you want us to believe that you've got our backs no matter what happens at the job. And I understand the confusion that most men feel when women send mixed messages sexually.

You get married, have kids, and forget that we are visual; we *love* what we married. And if you want the full support of your man, not every double whopper with cheese can be your friend.

Please, ladies, give me a chance before you turn me off.

I know men can be jerks. But I'm not talking about those men. (Hopefully, the last two chapters addressed stuff your man needs to hear.) I'm not even talking about the man who wants you to look like J.Lo but lets himself look like Rerun from *What's Happening!* I'm talking about the man who watches the kids so you can go do cardio. But you don't. The man who takes you to nice restaurants. But you still order what you did in high school.

So ladies, let us begin to construct your blueprint for sex. In order to turn around your sexual relationship with your man, you have to be honest with yourself when you are addressing the following issues. Otherwise, none of this will work.

Why are you no longer doing those things to keep him that you did to get him?

And when I say keep *him*, ladies, please understand that I'm *not* talking about the man who needs to practice some self-control or has a performance-based mentality.

You need to understand that a man will get up early and work late to take care of the woman who makes him feel like a king. A king in the bedroom. A king in front of your parents. A king in front of your girlfriends. And a king when he comes home to his wife. And if all you're hearing now is "weakness," you're not giving me a chance. Ladies, if you don't make your man feel like a king, he'll feel powerless in the world—a world full of deadlines, full of temptations; a world where some younger guy is the new heat at the office. He'll feel *powerless*; and you're the only one who can make him feel like his life is worth living. A woman's tongue is perhaps the most powerful influence on a man—more than his job, more than his environment, more than his future. What his woman does or doesn't say to him affects him like nothing else in his world. The tone and essence of a woman has a dynamic to it that pierces through your heart more than anything any other human can say. To a man, our boss telling us in front of the whole staff that we are fired is like a whisper compared to being cussed out or condemned by a woman. And if you are an African-American woman who seems to have her PhD in neck rolling and finger pointing, your actions and words will cut into the boy that we were, the child who was neglected, the teenager who had pimples and acne and who didn't fit in. That cussing out session speaks to every season of a man's life and reinforces what our mama said, reinforces what our auntie said, reinforces what everybody said to us, in just that one moment.

But that same black woman, because she's gifted with these nurturing hands and this nurturing touch, when she says, "Baby, don't worry about it" and she rubs our head and says, "I love you," she can make us forget every dark thing in our lives. A woman can speak life to her man or she can speak death. A good woman who speaks life to her man will have him trying to do things he can't even do. She can have a man trying to jump off buildings, to wear clothes that don't even fit, to put on a toupee or get his teeth fixed. He could be fifty and all of a sudden he got braces. All because his woman told him he should. A woman who tells her man he ain't nothing, who seems more emotionally connected to her friends, her family, everybody else's life, can make her man very small and make him start looking for love in the wrong places.

Women need to know that you don't always just have to sex your man down for him to feel covered. Because he probably had that before he married you. But he didn't marry the freaks. When he pulled out the ring it was because something about you spoke deeper to him. But at some point you stopped speaking deeper to him. He may have had something to do with that, but if you keep speaking life to him you can speak him back to health.

Ladies, when a man lies with his wife, he receives nourishment that penetrates the deepest, most broken, most vulnerable part of his soul. At a level of emotion that fills every area of his being. He forgets the world that was cruel for ten hours, the hopelessness he feels about his future. He is one with the divinely ordained creature who shares his last name and carries the gift that fulfills him like nothing else in this world. But when he's lying not with his wife but a girl he says he "really, really" cares for, he's giving you his best impersonation of a squirrel. Hope you get it. But back to marriage.

Ladies, when you take sex away from him or play games
with it, using it for control, you not only violate his greatest
love language, you also betray him as your soul mate.

Sickness, changes after giving birth, unaddressed emotional
issues—all these should be taken into consideration when a couple confronts a challenge in their sexual relationship. But to take
the attitude that your man should simply accept that you are
now married with kids, that you like your doughnuts at night,
and that there's more cushion for the pushin', is unfair. Let's
take a look at 1 Corinthians 7:1–4 real quick.

> Now concerning the things about which you wrote, it is
> good for a man not to touch a woman. But because of
> immoralities, each man is to have his own wife, and each
> woman is to have her own husband. The husband must
> fulfill his duty to his wife, and likewise also the wife to
> her husband. The wife does not have authority over her
> own body, but the husband does; and likewise also the
> husband does not have authority over his own body, but
> the wife does.

See, it's equal! This isn't that stupid "woman should submit"
crap. No, this is both of y'all being sold out in love to each other.
So, ladies, you need to think about sex more. Talk about sex
more. If you want things to improve, you simply can't get away
from this fact. It won't make you a loose female, it won't take
away from your high image, but it will bring you closer to your
man. Still be you, but talk to him; he'll love it.

Because of my mistakes in school, I always wanted to give my
kids the best education money could buy. So my kids attend a
pretty good private school here in Texas. After *The Oprah Winfrey Show* on which I talked about my past with pornography, the
kids had a field trip that Tammy couldn't attend, so I filled in (as

I should). One of the moms had seen the show. She told me how impressed she was to see me talk so transparently about the sort of things a lot of her friends had gone through. Then she confidently added, "Even though my husband is not involved in that."

"How do you know?" I asked.

" 'Cause he would never do that!" she said.

Again I asked, "How do you know? Have you ever talked to him about pornography?"

"No," she said.

"Do you and your husband talk about sexual issues?"

"No, not really."

"If you were to ask him if he's fulfilled in his relationship sexually, what do you think he would say?"

"I don't know."

Boo, you *want* to know. You *need* to know. I promise you, it *is* his love language. Not the only one, but certainly one of the main ones. Men look at women walking by. We notice breasts, bottoms, lips, hair. Again, self-control is important, but we love women. So for his sake and yours, talk to your man about sex.

It's not too late to be honest.

If there are some things you've done that you didn't like but you did them to catch the fish, then be honest about that. He's your best friend. Tell him that you want to learn along with him what you like. Apologize for the things you were not aware of that shut him down, and for the luggage you brought to the table because of how you learned about sex. He will feel blessed to know that he is sharing a part of you that no one else has ever shared. Tell him you are thankful he's the one helping you to learn about "you." And put some sugar on it.

I understand that some women have had horrible experiences

because they made themselves vulnerable to men who only used that vulnerability against them. So their attitude is, "I swear I'll never let a man hurt me again!" But what happened in the past doesn't mean that making yourself vulnerable won't work now; in the right relationship—one with a man who is truly caring, truly committed, truly loving—being vulnerable can be an important step to deep and genuine intimacy. Please don't let a jerk from your past spoil your relationship in the present.

In the Bible, a woman named Esther used her beauty to save her people. Married to the king, she used feminine influence to change his heart. She wasn't in there rolling her neck, snapping her fingers, and doing the "girlfriend Shaniqua" thing. Instead, she used beauty and brains to bring salvation to her people.

If your man isn't loving you in the way you need him to, put some sugar on it. Tell him you want to fall in love all over again; tell him you want to reconnect, to be one with him when you make love. That it's important to you, too. And then tell him what you need. Use those eyes. Hold his hand. Make him feel like you like him . . . again. He'll start brushing his teeth before he comes to bed; he'll shower first. He'll learn. Because he'll feel big; he'll feel loved. Not bringing your to-do list to the conversation won't make you weak. In fact, the change you bring about in him will prove your power. And you'll both win because of it.

Remember that he didn't marry a man; he married a woman. He didn't marry his mama, he married his boo, his baby. So *be* his baby. Let him know you find him attractive. Let him know that you think about sex more than he realizes.

My wife would tell me that at times during the day she thought about lovemaking, but by the time she picked up the kids, helped them with homework, and got them to bed, she had forgotten those thoughts.

As women, sex is so connected to your mind-set, to your

emotions. You can think about it, but the slightest thing can take that thought away.

So help your man. When you think about sex, text him. And say something sexy in the text. Or hit him with an e-mail. That way, even if it doesn't happen that night, he'll know that you were thinking of him. And if your day is filled with distractions, do what Tammy would do—ask for a rain check. Make it cute; say it with sugar on top, and let him know that you'll "hook him up" later. *Just make sure that later happens!*

Sometimes, when she has one of those weeks where she is "crazy busy," Tammy will simply rub up against me and say, "My week has been stressful. Thank you for understanding. I haven't forgotten about you. I love you." And I'm good.

The hurt we feel comes when everything else—the kids, the job, the friends—seems to get your time and attention; we feel forgotten, we feel undervalued. A soft, sexy kiss or a nice touch can go a long way.

Don't forget that we are visual.

We understand that some of the lingerie we buy for you is not the most comfortable. We realize that there are nightly rituals that women must go through to keep their hair and faces looking right for the next day; and *we* benefit from those rituals. We don't expect you to wear heels and a thong after you've been in the carpool lane and at soccer practice.

But we need—and beg—you to remember that we are stimulated by what we see. We didn't meet you with Noxzema on your face. When we picked you up for a movie, you didn't come out in sweats and house shoes. And please! Don't wear those thick, itchy pajamas to bed *every* night. Keep us attracted to you. Don't take us for granted just because we put a ring on it. When you stop carrying yourself the way you did when we first met each other, you make a man feel less valued. But if you carry yourself in a sexy way, we will see you as sexy. And how you carry yourself depends on how you see yourself. So, in the end, the issue is how you see you.

Women, talk to your men about how you feel about yourselves. If you are going through a season in life when you no longer feel sexy, not communicating will *not* make things better. You may say, "My man complains that I'm always talking. The last thing he wants is to talk about how I feel about my body or how I no longer feel attractive." If that's the case, you have to learn your man's beats.

The middle of the playoffs is probably not the time to ask if your butt looks bigger in those jeans. If your butt could help his team win, he'd love it just then. Since it can't, wait until the game is over to ask about your booty. In the middle of a fun, loving conversation—that's the time to ask. Learn his beats.

And make room for sex. Don't have the baby's toys lying on the bed or clothes that didn't get hung up stuck between the pillows. Make him think you've thought it through, that he's important enough for you to set the mood and the environment. No man—and hear me, *no* man—enjoys "I'm doing you a favor" sex from his wife. And if you want to make him angry, make him feel that he should be honored simply to see you naked. A devalued man is not a covered man. Keep your man covered.

It's unfair to ask your man to be tuned in to every detail of your life and then make him beg you to be with him sexually.

And ladies, you'll thank me for this one: Always remind him that you want to make him happy. Help him see your questions as being asked for his benefit, not simply for you to talk. Remember: Men want—and need—to feel big, especially about sex.

You are beautiful. You are created to be admired, adored, and found attractive. Men look at you like a work of art; when your man glances at you, he likes to be able to adore you, even from a distance. Whatever your size, your shape, your skin color, your age—he liked all of that when he met you. So *enjoy* being you. And don't be too hard on yourself. Being overly insecure can be less attractive to your man. For us, your strength is sexy, your confidence pulls us in; and watching you love you teaches us how to love you more! And if you are walking around all frowned up and mad about something with your lip poking out, don't be surprised if your man starts to pay less attention to you because men like to see their women as this heavenly Michelangelo creation. During the dating process when he looked at you he saw happy, but after you get married when he looks at you he sees mad. That's why you hear men telling other men "Don't get married because she'll turn evil!" You've got to try to hold on to that essence of happiness that you had in the beginning. And you hold on to it by learning his beats, not by making every conversation sound like an emergency. And communicate how you feel with your mouth, not your actions!

And please let me say that you cannot make everything an emotional issue. Yes, God created you emotional. But you are smarter than that. You are stronger than that. And sometimes you need to react more from your rational side than your emotional one. You can be strong; you can have the attitude that you want to see in him, the attitude that says, "I am going to live for my spouse's good." If a couple both have that mentality—that each exists for the other's sake—what stranger or outsider can compete with that?

No other man will ever be able to outdo me when it comes to telling my wife that she's the finest thing on the planet. No other man will ever outdo me when it comes to complimenting her eyes, her lips, or the way her hips move as she walks. And the same for her. She makes me feel big even though I'm five foot four. She tells me I'm sexy to her. She gives me things that keep me from being vulnerable to other women. So if we failed, it wouldn't be because we didn't invest ourselves completely in each other. People are always blown away that we've been married for as long as we have because she's my homie. We just act the fool together, messing around, having fun together.

This isn't a prehistoric attitude. This isn't a man trying to impose unrealistic expectations on the female population. And a lot of your perception is wrong: Not every man cheats. Some men bring their flesh under subjection every day. Yes, that's hard to do in an MTV, Internet culture. And it's even harder when a man doesn't feel loved and covered by his wife. Keep it spicy. As long as you don't feel uncomfortable, fulfill some of his goofy little fantasies. Ask him what he enjoys, but tailor it to fit your personality. Your sex drive may never match his, but when you do bless him, *bless* him!

Finally, knowing how overwhelming it can sometimes be for a woman to figure out a man sexually, I suggest to you what I suggested earlier to the men.

If your relationship with your husband isn't where it needs to be because you've lost something for him, ask God to give you back that something.

Maybe some old childhood experiences have come back to your mind. Maybe some stupid thing your husband did in the past keeps resurfacing in your memory. Or maybe just plain old life has changed some things in your heart and emotions. God created you as a sexual being. Since the "parts" are still there, trust Him to restart the engine.

I realize that men and women will never be the same sexually. Men can get an erection just sitting on a plane while it's landing. Women have a lot more strings connected to their desire and what turns them on. We also can't deny that far more women have been sexually abused in our society than men. That's a fact we have to work through. And that's one reason why, ladies, it is so important that the way you start off with a man sexually must be true to who you are. It's hard for your man to hear stories about your childhood when he first met you as "Ms. Give-It-to-Me-Baby." Don't be so desperate to get a man that you pretend to be well when your soul is sick. You never know; he could be an answer to the healing process. But if you go there, you must remember that he's a man. Sex will always be easier for him. No matter how Christian he is, it will be hard for a man to stay on the path of a healthy relationship when you are letting your sexuality do the driving.

Putting these things into motion won't be easy, ladies. And I know many women reading this are just too uncomfortable to have these types of gloves-off talks about sex. But ladies, I'm trying to help. I travel a lot internationally. I go to a lot of "hot spots" (Rio de Janeiro, Amsterdam) and I see more and more straight-laced men on those flights and at the hotels with women who have night-time occupations. Most of them are married, ladies. I know because they talk about it. I'm breaking the code here! Men are not staying satisfied in their marriages. Again, that is no excuse to make something wrong even worse, but you need to live with a clear conscience that you did the work, shared your heart, and made the sacrifices.

There will be times when you may even ask yourself if it's all worth it. But think on those times when your relationship has hit a sweet spot, when you and your man can exchange entire conversations in just a lingering glance, when your body surges with electricity just from his touch, when you can't think of anywhere else in the world you'd rather be than wrapped in his arms. And then think about those promises you made while standing in the presence of God that Saturday afternoon while your friends and family held back tears of joy. Remember all of that? Now what did you say about it being worth it?

Chapter Ten

PASSING THE BATON: THE BLUEPRINT FOR RELATIONSHIPS AND MARRIAGE

I n a world becoming quicker, more technical, and less personal, I often wonder whether the meaning of relationships stays the same. Do we continue to see relationships as a major fabric of society, institutions that allow human beings not just to coexist but also to walk through the pains and victories of life together? Or do we approach communication, friendships, love, marriage, and parenting like MySpace, Facebook, Twitter, or whatever new social network comes onto the scene that is "fresh" today but "old school" tomorrow? As we become more immediate in our daily lives, and the more that information and love seem to be just a click away, the more we seem to lose our ability to feel, express, and connect in a world where not every problem of the heart can be solved by searching Google.

One very important part of any building's blueprint is a clear indication of its emergency exits. Unfortunately, those exits are needed because accidents, fires, and terror threats are part of life's reality. Emergency exits give the individuals in the building a safe and well-planned way to escape danger. In a similar way, healthy relationships create a similar sense of security. They give us safe and well-planned ways of dealing with emergencies we can't handle on our own.

How horrible to have storms enter your life when you have no hand to hold on to or soft voice reminding you that these, too, shall pass!

I can always tell when I meet people who are unmarried and have no children. They often tend to be self-centered, career-driven, I/me/my–focused individuals. The same seems to go for people who have no siblings. Sharing and compromise tend to be very difficult for them. This reaffirms that nothing creates an individual who is "other"-centered like healthy, God-fearing relationships.

Men and women have lost their understanding of the power of relationships. We settle for standards we wouldn't encourage our children to accept. We've been programmed by various social and environmental conditions. Women who had domineering mothers find it difficult to embrace Judeo-Christian beliefs about being equal with their husbands but still allowing and trusting them to lead. Men who didn't see their fathers, or those who saw their fathers as nothing but financial providers, will make bringing home the bacon their only priority.

Then some women—some beautiful and some who don't feel as attractive—show no depth, insight, or understanding of who they are or where they are going, and they look entirely to a man to define all of that for them. Some men have been taught to never commit on a deep, emotional level to anything or anyone. They find themselves on their second and third marriages but choose to think that they simply have bad luck finding a good girl.

We could say so much about the importance of parents equipping their children with relationship skills that they can carry into adulthood. Most of us are trying to forget bad lessons we were taught years ago. Even lessons that we weren't intended to learn. And those who knew better often didn't give us the right information. Now we have a hard time getting the old wine out of new wine skins.

In Texas we celebrate a holiday called Juneteenth. (If you're from Texas and reading this right now, get your mind off the ribs, barbecued chicken, and *pataytuh* salad!) On June 19, 1865, slaves in Texas received news about the Emancipation Proclamation that set them free. Because Texas was still under Confederate control, the slaves had not yet been informed about the proclamation, even though it had been signed two years earlier. So for two years, they continued to live as slaves when in actuality they were free men; and until they received the news that slavery had been abolished, nothing changed. They continued as slaves because they just didn't have the information they needed. But once news of abolition reached them, everything changed.

You can see how important it is to equip our children and young people with the right knowledge, the right tools, the right information. They need to know the truth about themselves so they won't continue to act in a way that no longer fits who they truly are. No longer slaves to their past programming, but free to learn and love.

I am fascinated that, when I speak to youth groups around the country, I find more and more young men who have no idea how to carry a conversation with a young woman. And the same goes for young women—few of them know how to converse with a young man. I once had a young man stand with an attractive young lady, both of them pulled out from the audience. I asked him to show me how he would approach a young lady who he thought was someone he wanted to ask out. I promise you that it was not only like a sitcom, it was also like a funeral scene in a sad movie.

He said, "Pst . . . Pst . . . Say, little mama, what it do! Uh, I'm trying to holla at cha."

The young girl, about seventeen, just giggled and giggled. Then she looked at me and said, "I don't know what to say."

I said to her, "Tell him your name is not 'little mama' and you don't respond to a man calling you with 'Pst . . . Pst . . .'!"

Of course, afterward I sat with the young man, talking to him and teaching him some things, because you can't hold him accountable for what he doesn't know. But the fact is that our sons and daughters don't know how to be respected and approached in an honorable way. So they don't demand respect. *Fathers, where are you?*

The same group of young ladies was asked, "What do you like in a boy?" You might be surprised that their answers concerned what they got from a boy more than how he treated them. Of course, the young men focused mainly on the physical characteristics of a young lady—and some of that is to be expected from teenage boys with hormones flying off the wall. But if they are never taught more substantive things, they will grow up having shallow relationships and living shallow lives.

Given the way young men and women think, it is no surprise that young women dress to draw attention to the parts of their bodies that boys like because they want to be liked. And the same goes for the young man. If money and nice purses are what the cute popular girl in school wants, then the young man will sell weed, hustle on the corner, and do whatever brings quick loot to get that girl.

These same young people watch celebrities get married, only to divorce a few months, or even weeks, later. Relationships are viewed as disposable. "Till death do us part" seems like a throwback from a rerun of *Leave It to Beaver* and marriages that last for a long time come across as weird and Amish.

When you look at pop culture's image of the man in the house as seen on sitcoms and even some kid shows, the dad is dumb, aloof, or just flat-out "ig'nant"; the mom is the smart, aggressive decision maker for the home. I thank God for the smart, powerful women like my wife who are putting it down every day. I listen to Tammy. I seek her counsel. And I acknowledge when her way is the best way. However, she is not our leader. Still, her partnership makes my leadership stronger.

So look at us now. Our divorce rates have soared off the charts. The church no longer seems prepared to counterattack this explosion that has happened in the culture; our church leaders are getting divorced, having affairs, and no one is angry at sin anymore. It's "do what you feel." If she's fine, hit that. If your spouse is getting older, trade her in. And when I get tired of you, I want out. Want a free country? Well, here it is.

Let me just mention quickly one important point that we'll dig into later. When a society takes away the system that was put there to protect it from imploding, you have chaos and disorder. You have individuals who go by their own definitions of right and wrong. No God, no standard. Again, even a dumb kid from the streets like me can understand that.

If your faith doesn't agree with mine, you still must admit that the family is in trouble; we've reached a state of emergency. All of life revolves around a healthy, well-functioning family. Teachers can't teach their students well when the children's homes are not stable and reinforcing the standards of the classroom. Couples can't be expected to have long-lasting relationships when every show, every leader, and every other popular trend minimizes, makes fun of, and devalues relationships between one woman and one man. And when the blueprint keeps being changed, no clear way of survival remains in the plans for when tragedy strikes.

Let me share with you a story that may shed some light on a plan to help a long-standing foundation regain its rightful place in society. It may take a minute, so please stay with me.

My oldest son, when he was in high school, was running the 4x400. Those who know something about track realize the difference between this and other relays is that in this one each runner runs a lap himself. No distractions, just him and his opponents. My son ran the last leg that day. And he should have; after all, he's a Franklin (selfish plug!). His team looked good. Comparing them to the other schools, it looked like an easy win.

The first runner took his position. Some of the other dads and I were sitting in the stands, proudly watching our boys. The gun went off. The first runner on my son's team took an incredible lead. He was killing the other boys. I offered to get some sodas for the other dads because this race already seemed to be in the bag.

The runner turned the final corner and we get to the passing of the baton. Anyone who knows track realizes that the most difficult yet beautiful part of any relay is the passing of the baton. It has to be seamless, perfect. And when it's done right, it's one of the most graceful things in athletics. So the runner came down the final stretch, with a great lead, and he passed the baton; and it was perfect!

The second runner began to enjoy the lead created for him by someone else's hard work; he got comfortable leading and didn't pay attention to what he was doing. And when he got to the second turn, this fool dropped the baton! The coaches lost it. The other runners lost it. The dads lost it. (Some of the dads used words I can't include in this book!) Because it had rained earlier that day, the track was muddy and had debris on it. So the runner picked up a late, dropped, and dirty baton. And now the rest of the team had to run harder and faster just to get back in the race.

My father gave me a late, dropped, and dirty baton. He didn't teach me about manhood. He never modeled how to treat a woman for me. He didn't give me a blueprint showing how to be a daddy. So I had to run harder. I fell on my own, messed up relationships on my own, and finally learned how to treat my wife on my own. Because the baton wasn't passed to me cleanly, I had to run harder and faster just to get back in the race. As a matter of fact, my dad wasn't even at the track to watch me run, much less to help me win.

It's the same for relationships. Many of us were given bad batons. Dirty batons. Dropped batons. Mama hated men, so the daughter hates men. Daddy had kids all over town, so the son does, too. Daughter saw mama play games with men, dating only men who gave her financial security and having several boyfriends at once. "This is your play uncle coming over to visit," she would explain. Now the daughter runs her own lap the same way. And we pass the baton from generation to generation. Creating a steady stream of losers rather than winners.

Interestingly, those of us handed bad batons know the pain that comes with them. We know the frustration of "running in the dark" as well as the bitterness and failure we feel because we can't keep a good relationship. Or because we keep finding ourselves in bad ones. So the question is, *Why?* Why do we—*we who have run with limps most of our lives*—continue to pass late, dropped, and dirty batons?

We can't forget that it's not a sprint, but a relay.

You see, sprints are all about the individual. They focus on individual performance and achievement. If you win, you stand alone and receive the praise; if you lose, you stand alone and receive the criticism. Relays, however, have to do with the labor and joint efforts of a team. A *community* of athletes working toward the same goal. What my son's young teammate forgot is that no matter how good a lead you begin with, if you don't run your lap well, the whole team suffers.

Continuing with the issue of selfishness, it is impossible to create a healthy team, a strong partnership between you and your spouse, someone you are dating, or even a friend, when the focal point becomes you and how everything benefits you. You hear it in arguments. "What about me?" one partner says. "Well," the other responds, "what about me?" Relationships built on self-satisfaction will never truly enrich the lives of the individuals in them. If you are the only one benefiting from a relationship, you lose, and so does everyone else.

It's important to understand that most decisions we make in order to benefit ourselves are based on how we feel. But, we must remember, feelings have no intellect. They cannot survive without being attached to a thought. So if your decisions begin to focus on others, you will find your feelings starting to adjust to your choices. They can be trained to come in line with your new way of thinking. So instead of how you feel determining how you think, your new way of thinking will determine how you feel. (Sound too deep? Trust me, it ain't!) Especially when your thinking becomes, "The race is *not* about me; we *both* have to cross the finish line together."

Many marriages have failed because of arguments and disagreements that could have been prevented if one of the partners had just chosen to lose so that the other could win. Isn't that what Army Pfc. Ross McGinnis did in 2006 when he lost his life jumping on a grenade to save the lives of four other soldiers in Iraq? Dying so others can live; losing so that someone else can win. Was *your* point so important, *your* feelings so much the focal point that you couldn't even hear the other person? Once our feelings get caught up in our disagreements, all rationale gets lost in translation and selfish human nature kicks in to overdrive as we seek first and foremost to defend ourselves—even from the ones we say we love. Is it *really* that serious, to lose your boo?

It is unfortunate how hard most people find simply saying, "I'm sorry." You know people like that. Folks who will go to the grave without ever having acknowledged their wrongs—and without ever having mended their broken relationships. When they *do* call, it's "Hey, I just called to say, 'Wassup?' We haven't talked in a while, so I was just calling . . . since you act like you can't call nobody." *What?* No! Acknowledging the hurt and pain you've caused doesn't come by making a generic phone call. To think it does is to add insult to the injury. When we don't address what we've done to others, we demonstrate the very essence of a cold, selfish soul.

Whether family or friends, saints or sinners—pride controls the heart.

So the grand question is, What's more important—being right or being one?

I once heard a great man say, "The reason God commands that marriage be 'till death do us part' is because it takes that long to get to know someone."

I will let you in on one of the most painful yet beneficial lessons I've learned in fourteen years of being a husband. But it's a lesson that's essential for the building of a strong and sturdy blueprint:

Marriage is designed to be a mirror.

Marriage is harder than any other relationship, I think, because your spouse becomes your mirror. And the mirror reveals your weaknesses; it reflects your shortcomings, your flaws, and even your failures. God intended it that way; your soul mate is part of God's plan to remodel your soul. Follow me.

If you've ever gone through a remodeling in your home, you

know it can be a dirty, dusty process. Remodeling is filled with delays, changes, discomfort, inconvenience, and even invasion. No one likes those things, but we all want the final product. New bathrooms, new kitchens, new basements. But the work of tearing out the old to replace it with the new can be long and hard.

And you didn't know your temper was that bad—that much in need of refurbishing—or that your fashion was too loud and bright until you got close to someone who revealed it. *(Thanks, baby!)* Because that's what mirrors do; they reveal. Soul mates reveal what needs to be remodeled . . . in your soul.

When faced with the tough arguments when a hole seems to be opening up right under you, remember to ask yourself, "Is this a deal breaker?" Is this fight, this conflict, big enough and serious enough to justify walking away from everything I've sowed into the relationship? Or does the value of this person trump my feelings about the situation?

It would be beautiful to have a mind-set of investing in our relationships with people, of hanging in there rather than throwing in the towel every time we hit bumps on life's road. We are so focused on our happiness that when people don't make us happy, they become disposable. Like condoms, they're for our temporary pleasure. And when we're finished with them, they get flushed with the moment . . . and the memory. Yes, relationships are work, and they don't come easy. But when your choices create a level of joy in the person you claim to love and care for, your ROI—the return on your investment—is priceless.

If my decision to be faithful to Tammy were ever to change, and I were to choose to step out of my marriage, not only would I be unfaithful to her, but I would also be unfaithful to my sons, to my daughters, to her family, to her circle of friends, and to the people who've supported my ministry over the years. One selfish act affects not only individuals; it affects whole communities. This isn't a sprint; it's a relay.

Don't have too much weight in the shoes.

After the race I heard the father of my son's teammate chastising the boy for wearing shoes that were not meant for the track. He had left his track shoes at home and instead brought some older ones that fit better. But the older shoes weighed him down and didn't have the right kind of gripping for the curves. So he couldn't run well. Having them longer didn't make them better for that race.

Isn't that like us? We wear things that are too heavy for the current relationship—things like past hurts, abusive relationships, and lack of trust. Instead of leaving past problems in the past where they belong so that the new relationship has a fair chance of succeeding, we bring our old laundry into the present. We make today's relationship carry burdens created by yesterday's. And we have too much weight in our shoes.

Sometimes we bring such a victimized mentality into our relationships that the other person ends up paying for the mistakes of someone they've never even met. We wear that kind of mentality because it fits better, because we've worn it for so long. Not because it's good for us. It's just more familiar, more comfortable. So now new people become the object of our past frustrations. But nothing they can ever do will pay off the other person's debt.

Those who bring old laundry into new relationships probably have no idea how many potentially great relationships they've destroyed because of the climate they created. A climate in which the seed of friendship finds it almost impossible to grow; a negative climate, a judgmental climate; since it's old laundry, a stinky climate, a climate in which every man and woman is seen as just like all the others who've gone before; a climate in which everyone is suspected of having a hidden agenda. *Please!* Sometimes these folks even use their past as a tool to destroy relationships in an intentional attempt to save themselves the trauma of what they assume will end up being another heartbreak. Since they already know the other person will end up abandoning them, they might as well go ahead and get it over with. So they create arguments and fights as a means of self-preservation.

No fun, no excitement, and it's their own fault.

People who carry a lot of emotional weight need to understand something very important: We're getting tired of you. Yes. I say this for all the people who don't have the courage to hang up the phone on you complaining about the same thing over and over again. You ruin every party, every movie night, every sad song that comes on the radio.

We are tired of seeing you tear up the pew at church and fall all out every time the choir sings "Never Would Have Made It." And we are tired of picking you up from the altar *every* Sunday. With all of the Bible studies and Scripture you've quoted, we should have seen some changes by now. But you don't realize, my dear brother or sister, that misery has become your god. It ministers to you. You're more comfortable making people feel your pain than taking a chance on being happy and strong. So you end up like a lot of the older people in some of our communities—negative and cynical about everything and everybody. You tear down people to feel better about the fact that you never dared to dream, never dared to leave your front yard. We're getting tired of you. So either do your business or get off the pot.

We have a choice about our future—*we can either run bitter or run better.*

Bitter runners make the whole team miserable. A bitter athlete is like a runner who shows up to run a sprint wearing boots, a hooded sweater, gloves, and corduroy jeans. She is weighed down by unnecessary clothing that hinders her from running the best race. World-class sprinters wear the least clothing possible. The less you wear, the lighter you are for your event. Ancient

Olympians even ran in the nude! Imagine that! So bitterness must be seen the same way—as a hindrance to your future. It interferes with your efforts to run life's race; it prevents you from realizing your potential to trust, to love, to believe.

So you can run bitter. Or you can run better. You can forgive those who caused the pain that has haunted you throughout life. You can lay aside the confusion you've carried from relationship to relationship. You can take the wounds from your past and use them as the fuel you need to propel you into the future—the future that God has designed for you, the future in which He has big plans for you.

The bad can be used for good. But you have to make the choice. A choice based not on your feelings but on truth. Because, if you don't mind my going here for a moment, it takes a choice to trust the sovereignty of God. It takes a choice to believe that nothing good, bad, or ugly comes into your life without first passing through His hands (remember that?). And when you see that, you know that your pain serves a divine purpose. And you love differently, even though all you've known was hate. I dare you to believe this truth!

And remember: The person who most needs you to forgive those who've wronged you is you.

Which leads to a final thought: Why didn't the coach notice that the young man didn't have on the right shoes? Why let him compete at a high level when he didn't have the right equipment to succeed?

Be on the lookout for bad coaching.

You'll love this one. When the track meet was over, I began reflecting on some things that could have been done differently. For one thing, I realized that my son's school doesn't have a track. Hmm . . . The plot thickens. My son's track coach uses orange construction cones and chalk to create lanes in the grass. You get it? How in the world can a track team be expected to practice all week on grass and then compete on a real track with kids who spend their time training on the real thing? The coach should have used his relationships with nearby schools to get his team on a real track so they would be ready when the time for competition came.

Many of us are like athletes who have not trained in the right environment. And so we're not set up, not prepared to have winning relationships. We were raised in single-parent homes to such an extent that we thought a kid was either weird or rich if he had *both* a dad *and* a mom in his home. For most of us, divorce was the norm. We almost never—and some of us *never ever*—saw healthy, loving marriages or families when we were growing up. That's why we loved, and still love, *The Cosby Show*. I still love turning on Nick at Nite and catching reruns of a family I dreamed about having as a young kid. For thirty minutes, we escaped our hellish situations and imagined ourselves with a dad and mom like Heathcliff and Clair.

Then, when the show was over, we went back to our drunk uncles who came by the house to borrow money. Our mothers were in the other room on the phone arguing with our fathers for money to get some back-to-school clothes. We went back to family members who hated one another, to stepdads who taught us how to smoke a joint and told us never to fall in love because love was for punk boys. These were our coaches, our role models. The pimp, the crazy man who swept the driveway on Saturday mornings for some of grandmama's tea cakes. *(Some of y'all are too young to know what tea cakes are!)* These were our architects, our coaches, our teachers. We failed at relationships because we lived like we saw them living, doing what we saw them doing. And we grew up teaching the same lessons to our kids.

So the baton continues to be dropped. Just like that day at

the track. What did the rest of the runners on the team that day do with the dropped baton?

I watched my son because how he responded at that moment would show me what kind of coach I'd been to him. Would he get angry and walk off the field? Would he complain the rest of the day about what the other runner had done wrong? What would he do?

As a father, I needed to know.

He started to stretch. He started to warm up his body by jumping up and down, raising one hand over the other. He was repositioning himself to get back in the race. *Yes!* Whatever happened in your life yesterday, you can reposition yourself today.

You see, how you see the problem is the problem.

What looked like just another poor slum village in Calcutta to you and me ended up being an incredible missionary field . . . for Mother Teresa.

When black poets in the 1920s feared rejection because of their skin color, Langston Hughes saw the situation as an opportunity, saying, "If white people are pleased we are glad. If they are not, it doesn't matter. We know we are beautiful. And ugly too." (In a piece from 1926 called "The Negro Artist and the Racial Mountain.")

And in 1934 a youth group thought he was too worldly. But Billy Graham went on to become one of the most famous people of the twentieth century and to preach to more men and women across the globe than any other Christian. Ever.

And somebody like me—somebody who never had a coach in the home, never saw a healthy marriage modeled as a kid—is now a father. A husband. A friend. A leader. And a servant.

Because I repositioned myself to get back in the race. No matter how many times you've been surrounded by negative influences, this is your time, your life. You have the opportunity to reposition yourself, to stop blaming those who came before you, to stop running bitter, to stop carrying burdens that no longer belong there, and to realize that you've been called to run a race that no one else can run but you.

I feel like preaching, but I won't!

Good track coaches have their runners run sprints, and they time them. The coach stands at the end of the track and clocks them as they pass by. You know what he's doing? He's looking for his fastest runner. The one he will put on the last leg of the relay in case somebody drops the baton. He needs someone bringing it home who has enough speed to get back in the race.

It is no coincidence that you were born when you were born or how you were born. And all the difficulties you've been through in life serve a purpose. Your "coach" knows your times and he puts his fastest runners at the end. To get the team back in the race.

Your mother may have dropped the baton, but God has you running the last leg to get your family back in the race. Your marriage doesn't have to end the same way. Your dad may have been a womanizer who dropped the baton. But God knows your time is fast enough to run your leg without making the mistakes your father made. All the pain you've endured has conditioned you for the race your coach knew you would need to run. That, my people, is what the pain is for. Not to kill you or take you out, but to make you a beast on life's track. A winner, a champion. So you won't fall to pieces at every disappointment. Or walk out whenever marriage is no longer fun.

A good coach always puts his fastest runners at the end. Just in case somebody drops the baton. But you need not—by God's grace, *will* not—drop the baton. Because in Christ, you have repositioned yourself to get back in the race. Not just to finish, but to win.

By the way, my son's team didn't win that race; even better, though, my son won my heart and affirmed my role as a coach.

I pray that you've been blessed by my attempt to remind you how important we are *for* each other and *to* each other; how our healthy relationships, especially our healthy families, serve as the only true foundation for a healthy society that sees us not in terms of color or creed but as people created to live life together.

We must not forget that we are links in the great chain of human history, that our actions and choices can destroy what comes after us. Because it only takes one weak link. A group of young campers went hiking inside a cave. The farther they went inside the cave, the darker it got. Soon the kids became lost in the darkness. And hours turned into days. After several days, an emergency rescue team went in to find the children. Sadly, after hours and hours, they found the bodies of the young children huddled together as if they were keeping themselves warm in the cold darkness. When they began identifying the bodies by going through the kids' backpacks, they discovered that one of the kids had had a flashlight in his pack. Apparently, in the midst of being lost, he panicked and forgot that he had with him a way to escape the darkness. Imagine the lives that could have been saved that day if that young camper had only remembered the light he had in his backpack, a light that could have prevented tragedy. But he forgot he had the light, and many lives were lost.

What about all the people in your life, in your family, on your job, lying next to you, who could be saved from heartache, despair, and an eternity separated from God if you'd let your own light shine?

May no one be lost forever in darkness because we never used the light we've received!

Chapter Eleven

IT TAKES A WHOLE NATION: THE BLUEPRINT FOR PARENTS

Wow! Words don't even seem sufficient to express how I feel about this subject. Since I started work on this book, I've looked forward with much anticipation to writing this chapter. Parenting is my greatest passion and heaviest burden. Being daddy is my proudest accomplishment.

Make no mistake: Being a parent is no doubt the hardest, most invasive role ever created for man or woman. There are no Grammys for daddies, no Nobel Prizes for mommies. Nothing in life makes me feel so dumb and weak as being a father. It is definitely a role I've had to mature into. But I'm so glad that I didn't give up and quit before I had the chance to see the fruit of my desire to learn.

To know my past is to understand why my heart beats so vigorously for my children. At this very moment, as I write these words, my mind fills with memories and emotions that make my fingers tremble as I type. I became a dad with no blueprint, no coach. A flawed, confused, and still-learning dad, one blown away at having become a father. One of my close childhood friends told me one night that even in my twenties as a young dad myself and doing a lot wrong, my conversation back then was about how much I wanted my own family, about how much I wanted to be a father.

People, I can't begin to tell you the anger and frustration that I still deal with daily from not having had my father and mother parent me. I've had to deal with psychological issues about not being good enough, about who I really am, and about my plan in life, my blueprint, if you will. My mother and father left me to be adopted, so I deal with abandonment issues. I never heard, "Son, I'm proud of you," so I deal with acceptance issues. And as I said earlier, it is hard to see God's love as a father when you've never had one.

As I write this chapter, I'm in a hotel room in Houston, Texas. My biological father lives here. But I don't even know the man. I haven't seen him in years. And when I did see him, it was at a concert in Houston after my first album came out. He showed up to get some love from me. He brought his kids and told them, "Y'all go over there and say hi to your brother." This book would get an R rating if I wrote the words and emotions that went through my mind when he had the audacity to do me like that. No investment, no wisdom, no piano practices, but now he shows up wanting some love.

Parenting is not a Ferris wheel; you don't just jump in whenever you want to. You're on it for the whole ride. When my first child's mother told me she was pregnant, I was seventeen. I had no money, I was already failing out of school, and for several months I was homeless. But I knew innately that this child was someone for whom I had to take responsibility. I didn't have much. And when a child is born outside of marriage, there will be some conflicts between the parents. Not because they are bad people, but because being an adult comes to them without notice. So they are forced to be what they didn't choose to be. But even though those realities about my childhood were there, and I was now a child with a child, the pain of my past could not be inflicted on this child who didn't ask to be here.

When Tammy and I got married, she had a six-year-old daughter. When I knew that Tammy was the gift God had planned for me, being a father to her daughter was a no-brainer. When I married her, I married her daughter. I adopted her, changed her name, and was honored to become her blueprint for how a man is to love his children.

Tammy and I have had two children together, so I went from having hardly any family of my own to having a wife and four kids almost overnight.

I travel with my kids. They had passports by the time they were eight. We even home-schooled them for a couple of years so they could be closer to me when I was traveling a lot. I spank my kids. Now if you feel like calling child protective services on me, just know that I have bail money in a shoe box under my bed. But please understand, I ain't scared to tell you that I spank my kids. Because I don't want them growing up spanking me, I spank my kids.

And as much as I have physically disciplined my kids, I love and listen even more. I apologize to my kids when I get something wrong. If I don't, how else will they learn that skill? I teach my daughters not to chase boys, that boys should always come to them. And I teach my sons not to call women out of their names, no matter what the culture says about using words like "b*tch" and making them empowering. We don't do that. We revere young women; we open doors, we don't belittle.

I teach my young son that leading a home is not telling everyone what to do. Being a leader means being the first one up and the last one to bed. You, not your wife, take the bullet for your family. You, not your wife, lay your life down if necessary.

The climate of the home, the direction of the home, the safety of the home, and the failure of the home falls on the man.

My eight-year-old son took my wife on a date when I was out of town once. He has a crush on Tammy, so he couldn't wait until I left the house to get her all to himself. I have to remind him, "She's not *your* woman, she's *mine*." But he doesn't listen.

She told me he put the whole thing together. Someone had given him a gift card from the Cheesecake Factory, so he told her he wanted to take her out to eat. Tammy said he dressed himself, put the gift card in his wallet, opened the car door for her, and asked her if he could sit in the front because he's not supposed to sit in the front yet. While they were driving, he asked her, "So, what do you want to talk about?" And Tammy, trying to keep her inner laughter about the whole experience from coming out, asked him, "Well, would you like to hold my hand?" He said, "I was just thinking that!" Finally, when they got to the restaurant, he said, "I wanna come open your door, but I'm not allowed to be in the parking lot by myself." *Cute!* By now my wife is dying inside. He reached for her hand as they walked inside. And then she says she realized, "He's doing everything he sees his father do." He ordered bottled water like I do; he wanted a window table like I do. He was doing everything he'd seen his father do. Wow!

Is that not what we're missing? Ladies, I know it's frustrating when you see men failing to take care of their responsibilities or failing to cover you from danger, but most of us do what we saw our fathers do. And men complain that women have become more aggressive, but they're just doing what they saw mama do. There will always be exceptions, but for the most part our parents program what we like, how we think, and what we will be. Or what we *think* we can be.

I have a passion for young America. I've been blessed to have the chance to speak at major universities and churches all across this country. I see the kids at the mall, when they come over to the house for special events, when they walk down the street, and in parking lots with their friends. They look lost. They seem angry. Their countenance says, "I hate you and anyone else who don't like it!" They're mad at the world. And they should be.

I would be angry, too, if somebody invited me to come to Russia to speak, but when I got there no one was at the airport to pick me up. Or if they never sent an itinerary. Or if, when I tried to come home, I realized my ticket was one-way. Now, you may say, "But Kirk, you should have gotten most of that information before you got there." True. But what if it was somebody I trusted, somebody I had a relationship with? What if they said they loved me? Would I be wrong to trust them? To take them at their word? Now I'm stuck. No direction, no plan, and no way home. So I'm in Russia, but I'm not enjoying it because I don't know where I am. *(Sorry, just had a painful moment thinking about my own life!)* And the only reason I'm here is because somebody else invited me.

This generation has been dropped off. It's been abandoned by parents who, like you and me, didn't keep their word. Parents who promised to be there, but then were nowhere to be found. Parents who are so busy trying to keep their youth, their financial portfolio healthy, their careers and personal lives from failing—even trying to keep up with celebrities on TV—that their children have no idea where they are.

Teachers call for conferences, and we go with negative attitudes because we had to take off to be there. And if the teacher says anything we disagree with, we simply become defensive, arguing our points rather than communicating, rather than trying to understand. And our children suffer because we don't partner with their teachers.

Our children ask for our attention, and we make them feel ashamed because we've been at work all day.

We respond in anger and disappointment when our children get in trouble with the police, but we aren't nosy enough to ask them hard questions about their friends.

We drop them off at church and expect the youth pastor to fix everything in two hours once a week.

We are reactive, not proactive, with their failures, mistakes, and temptations. So they disconnect; they don't ask us to come to the church play; they don't want our advice because all we do is criticize and point out how stupid their decisions are. So when they take their hearts and walk out the door and into the world, just remember, you helped open it.

I've come to understand that no ten-year-old girl says to herself when thinking about her future, "When I grow up, I want to get pregnant by a guy who leaves me; then I want to drop out of school, get my GED from the library, and work a minimum wage job for the rest of my life." I realize that many, many women started out their lives as young parents from unplanned pregnancies and have gone on to be incredibly successful. But without strong family support systems and committed coparent relationships with the fathers, those success stories wouldn't have happened. And they are the exception, not the rule.

So with shattered dreams and a new plan that has now become the young lady's reality, she runs her race. And she is bitter. Mad because this is not how the dream was supposed to go. No health care; fighting for child support; being the young lady who finds it hard to date because she's got a baby; always having to look at a child who resembles the man who left, the one who isn't around. So she spends a lot of time angry, sometimes not even realizing it.

Same for the father. He was on his way to college. Football. Or maybe he was just an immature young kid trying to figure out his own life. But now he's faced with trying to figure out two—really *three*—lives. So now he's angry with her. "She" ruined his dreams. "She" is the reason his mama's baby boy didn't get to finish college. "She" is the reason for the pressure and stress he's under. And now he hates her; he hates life. Now he runs life's race not better but bitter.

So the child grows up under a cloud of anger, bitterness, and frustration. And in that constant environment, the child begins to take on the character of the parents. Always angry parent; always angry child.

And the level of divorce in our society not only leaves children feeling like they've been dropped off in another country, it also leaves them cynical about marriage. Most of these kids don't want to get married! Would you? If your father feels like his wife is getting too old and leaves her for a young thang, what is committed about that? When parents divorce and remarry, divorce and remarry, and so on, like they're changing hairstyles or underwear, what is attractive about that? Why would our kids want to do it? They would rather live together than put labels on each other, to create whatever so-called protective barriers they can to minimize collateral damage. They don't feel safe; they don't feel secure. And the thought of two people lasting forever is no more realistic than Renée Zellweger telling Tom Cruise, "You had me at 'Hello.'" (*Jerry Maguire,* people.)

Even Maria Kefalas, a well-known feminist and sociologist, has admitted that divorce has deeper psychological effects (I call them *scars*) on children than the so-called experts used to think. So even the pros are acknowledging what we victims have known for years. A child is built to survive on what *both* parents—not just one—have inside them. It doesn't take a degree to figure that out; the research is right next to you—at malls, walking the streets, hanging out in parking lots, and disrespecting your home.

It can be even worse when both parents stay in the home but with no engagement, no interaction, no affection, no love. Then the children don't see love modeled; they just see provi-

sion. Provision is a great thing. But a smaller home, a less expensive car, and more *you* would make a child much happier. Because,
honestly, that house and car were really for you. So maybe most
of us are only doing what we saw done; or maybe we choose to
be foolish and self-centered because all of us are naturally selfish.
Nothing will change until we recognize this important fact:
We've let these kids down. From television to radio, pulpits to parents, we have failed this generation. They've become a second
thought, second-class people in our society. We view them with
an "oh yeah, the kids" afterthought mentality; all of us, that is,
except for marketers who understand their buying power, gangs
who look to fill in the hole left by absent fathers, and lovers who
prey on people with esteem issues reinforced in homes where
they were never told who they are or what to look out for.

We have failed them. The home has failed them. The community has failed them. The church has failed them. This nation
is failing them.

We felt anger for our soldiers when they were sent to fight in
Iraq without the proper armor; we should feel that same kind of
anger about what we are doing to our children. They are being
sent out into a war without the proper armor. But the truth is,
it's easier to be angry about someone else's mistakes rather than
about our own.

As God is the architect, so the parent is the general contractor. It's the parent's job to execute the plans. To find the right
plumber, a qualified electrician, a skilled carpenter. To make sure
the finished work resembles the blueprint. He should never devi-
ate from the plans, should never come up with his own design
for the house. His job is to fulfill his call; to build a masterpiece
that will make the architect and the owners of the home proud.
But as we see these buildings fail and fall, we see a great disconnect between what the blueprint calls for and what gets built in
real life. So let's set about building your blueprint for parenting.

Parenting is not an option.

When you have a child, you make an unspoken pledge. You say, "I am pledging myself to make my child's well-being, development of a positive mind-set, and spiritual and emotional health my top priority. If my child loses, I lose; if my child wins, I win." To not have that mind-set is to violate the contract, to change your mind on a purchase that can't be returned.

When you have a child, your life and priorities must shift. Not that you can't have a life. But the success of your life shouldn't come at the cost of the child. A child can't be dropped in on; a child is not someone you pencil in, someone you put off on grandma to take care of. *A child is a call you take every time the phone rings.*

Our lives should have some absolutes, some things that never change. Rather than working them around everything else, everything else should be worked around them. Your children must be one of those absolutes. Career decisions must be made around those absolutes. Personal plans must be built around those absolutes. Your children should never feel that they are getting in the way of your dreams, your goals, your religion, your happiness. You made a decision to have them. Even if the pregnancy was unplanned, the child is still a gift from God. Understand: There may be illegitimate relationships but never illegitimate children.

Since little Jerome is going to grow up someday, you have to count the cost.

We can get so enamored with the idea of having cute little kids that we're not careful to remember that the cute little baby we laugh at for saying curse words he heard us say won't be so cute when he curses you out for real. Little Jerome *does* grow up. That's what happened with my relationship with Gertrude. She just didn't understand me turning from a boy to a teenager who wanted to talk to girls on the phone. I was no longer cute little Kirk; in her mind I became a problem child.

And as for the parent who can't let it go? You know who you are. You may have gotten pregnant in high school, so you didn't get to cheer or go to the prom. You didn't go to college to play football. You didn't get drafted in the NFL. And everything your child does is really your opportunity—to do it or to do it again.

We see you at the football games. You know every cheer. You're on the sidelines fixing her makeup between cheers. You're down there next to the coaches, giving suggestions on what plays to run. You curse out the referee. You go to the mall with little Molly and her girlfriends. When Molly gets her hair cut, you surprise her with your new hairdo. And Dad, your son's girlfriend feels uncomfortable because you suck your teeth and call her "cutie pie" when she comes over. You smother your kids. You overparent. They don't even know how to fall, because you won't let them. So they never learn how to get up. I lovingly say to you the same thing I would say to the bald-headed man who rocks a long ponytail: *Let it go!*

Friendship with your children is not the engine but the caboose. In other words, friendship with your child is the by-product of a good relationship with your child, not the basis of it. What drives your relationship with your child isn't how much you kick it with them, not how much you laugh and tell jokes with them. But as a general contractor, the question is how well you've laid the foundation. At times the foundation gets laid by discipline, by tough love, by saying no, and by understanding that their not always liking you doesn't mean their not always loving you.

I found this also in my own life with Tammy's daughter— now my daughter Carrington. I believe that most stepparents never want to be viewed as step, but real. So we struggle inside with that sense of insecurity and we overcompensate. We don't want the child to dislike us. So we rarely say no. We overdo the friendship. We sometimes let the child get away with things we know aren't right. And then after years of parenting out of fear and performance, we begin to see holes in the child's character, in their sense of respect, in understanding roles; and we get mad when we demand something but they don't know how to give it because we haven't been consistent as a parent. It is not the child's fault; it is ours.

When Carrington grew older, I asked her forgiveness because I wasn't always stern enough with her because I didn't want her to reject me. Being twenty and in college on her own, she told me that she wished I had been sterner. She actually wanted discipline, even if she didn't "want" it.

Kids want structure. They *need* structure. They don't need to be falling out in the grocery store when they can't get the Fruity Pebbles. They don't need to raise their voices at you when you reinforce their curfew. *You* pay the bills in the house. *You* clipped those coupons all afternoon. *You* are the one saving for their college and to help them realize those future dreams they will have. You deserve respect. You've earned respect. And I promise: It will be hard for them to give it to you when all they see is their friend.

They don't always need a buddy; they need a leader. They need someone to set the tone for the home and encourage everyone else to step in line with that tone. How else will they learn to respect authority? How will they learn how to lead if not by seeing it every day at home?

Even if you're a single parent, you're called to lead your home. Don't parent out of guilt, trying to make it up to the child because daddy is not around or mama got married to some guy who has money. Your children are wired by God to interpret love. They know that love is around them, even in a one-bedroom apartment. Even in the projects.

Make sure that your child is not a pawn of your own pain.
Love your children with what you have. Even if some pieces are missing. That's where your confidence in God kicks in. Remember that you are called and created to do this. Even in a mistake, God's unlimited power can give you grace to right your wrongs. Remember that how you start with your kids is how you'll end. With much prayer and learning, you can pick up the pieces and get it back together. But if you start off smoking around your kids, dogging out the other parent, drinking around your kids, and bringing your boyfriend or girlfriend around your kids, it will be very hard to *un*program things they have seen you do over and over again. They already have friends. They go to school with friends. They need a parent—when it's fun *and* when it isn't. Like is conditional, love isn't.

And for all of the stepparents who have felt this tension, I want to encourage you. Having a child who is *not* biologically mine has been one of the greatest joys in my life. She's my baby. She's my sweetie pie. (All of my children are.) And when she was born, God predestined me to be her daddy. That's my confidence. That's your confidence. Take your position. Even if the child doesn't live with you full-time. Or if the other parent is in the picture and your philosophies don't line up. You parent your house. You love with a big stick in your house. And trust the God of your destiny to give you the wisdom and power that you don't naturally have. They may not always like you, but they will come to love you.

Playing house hurts, it doesn't help.
Again, it's easy to understand why there has been such a drastic rise in the percentage of people living together rather than getting married. We watch Nick and Jessica, Mr. and Mrs. Hulk Hogan, and Jon and Kate (who have *eight*). And we say "no" to the idea and the heartache of marriage.

But those who believe that living together rather than getting married protects them from the harsh realities of daily life are only fooling themselves. As soon as the woman starts to make demands on the man—demands like fidelity, coming home every night, sharing bank accounts, and sharing responsibility for raising a child—and the man starts looking for his meal every evening and wants to live in an apartment that has only her name on the lease, the bubble bursts. And the "going through the back door" outlook on relationships and family kicks in.

You cannot cheat reality. The child *will* be affected by the "on and off" cycle that often goes with live-in relationships. And the child never gets to see commitment modeled. So the idea of sticking to something until the very end doesn't come naturally to the child; perhaps it will be learned later—hopefully, before it's too late.

Please watch what you say and do.

People, I want you to know that what our children hear us say and how they see us living is destroying this generation. Our influence has become raggedy, irresponsible, ghetto, and just downright immature. From what we name our kids, to what we teach our kids, to the things we expose our kids to, we are creating time bombs waiting to explode. They listen, they watch, and they learn.

After the election of President Obama, my kids came home from school the very next day with weird looks on their faces. Tammy and I asked them about their day, and they began to share with us some of the things other kids were saying about the election. Being part of only a handful of minorities at this private prep school, they went to school with a sense of pride at seeing the first African-American president ever elected in this country. But they were confused and discouraged by the responses of other kids that day. In the halls of the schools, people were saying, "Whoever voted for Obama, thank you very much for taking food out of my family's mouths! My dad has to pay extra money for lazy people who don't want to work!" These are eleven-year-olds! They don't know what they are talking about; they are simply repeating what they've heard—from other "Christian" parents.

There were several other situations like this across our city. One friend of mine had a conference with school administrators because one of the teachers was talking like this to her fourth-grade class. Blasting President Obama's views to little kids. Everyone in this country enjoys the freedom to have an opinion on any issue in our society, and to express it. And as a family, we don't agree with all of the president's views and policies. But with freedom comes responsibility.

Once another parent caught my son being mean to a little kid at lunch because of his religion. He didn't let the little boy sit with him and his buddies because the boy was Muslim. When the parent told me about the situation, I did what I hope the other child's father would have done if faced with the same situation. I told my son that being a Christian *never* gives you the right to embarrass others because of their beliefs. To not allow the boy to sit at the table with you doesn't make you a good Christian. It makes you a bad one.

Your racial views affect your children. Your spiritual views, and how you present them, affect your children. Your drinking affects your children. Your late-night tippin' affects your children. How you deal with your money, honey, affects your children.

Last, be careful what you speak into your child's life.
I remember once hearing my biological mother say to my adopted mother, "I didn't want a baby. I wanted to have an abortion, but you wouldn't let me!" I was thirteen years old . . . and

the memory is still so vivid that it's like I'm standing in the same place right now, feeling the same rush of horrific emotions. What did I hear? I heard I wasn't wanted. I wasn't welcomed onto this planet. That if my biological mother hadn't been *begged,* she would have thrown me away. That's why I am an advocate for life. There would have been no "Imagine Me" or "Stomp" or "Why We Sing" if she had gotten her way. All those songs would have been aborted, along with me.

When you have a child, your words are life and death to that child. They hang on to everything you say. If you tell them they are winners, they will believe you. If you tell them they aren't worth (fill in the blank), they will believe you. They are tape recorders made of clay. What you speak and how you mold them will establish their first steps on the way to their destiny.

I've heard parents call their kids "bad" as a term of endearment. When the little boy does something that's a little too mature for his age, they jokingly say, "Stop that with your little bad a**!" The programming process starts right then and there. You said it to him as a child, but he heard it as a man. When a little girl is a bit sensuous in some of her choices of clothes or mannerisms, we call her "fast." We think it's cute that she can do some of the new dances she's seen in music videos, and without realizing it, we celebrate something other than the best part of being a woman. It is not her curves or her ability to do the splits while bouncing up and down at age eight that we should be celebrating. We applaud the little girl, but she receives it as a woman.

You are there to bring out the best in them, to give them names that represent power and a sense of history—not something you saw on a liquor bottle. Not to tell them that they're going to be sorry like their daddies; not to vent your frustration on them because you're mad at their mothers for requesting back child support. You are there to help them find their voices. Not to remind them how proud you are of their siblings, all the things those siblings have accomplished, and how you wish they would be more like them. Help them to be the best them!

Please, let's start acting like adults! You are not your kids' peers. They are not your psychiatrists. Save your breakdowns and cursing matches for someone who can handle them. Stop being a punk and man up and regain your position as the leaders seeking this generation's well-being. As things now stand, we are creating a future of desensitized, untrusting, cynical, and numb children who have had to learn how to be teacher and child. Let's get it together! They are hungry for you to define them. To mold them. To reaffirm them. To write the blueprint for them to build on. You are the general contractor. The teacher. The life coach. You are the parent, and also the friend.

Love them. And please give them what we didn't have.

If you aren't ready in your life to make that type of commitment and decision, that's perfectly okay. Responsible people take life-altering decisions seriously and make them soberly. And your reason for having a child shouldn't be that you're lonely. I read an article in a popular music magazine about a rapper whose mom asked him to have a baby so she could raise it *because she was lonely*. That might seem endearing and heart-warming from a distance, but in fact it is irresponsible and self-destructive.

Holidays and special events cannot be the times when we choose to be engaged, involved parents. Even after divorce or the choice not to marry the other parent, this "absolute" should never be affected. I will say it again just to make sure I'm heard: Your children should never suffer unnecessarily because of choices you thought were best for you.

So you ask God to give you what you don't have naturally, what you never saw modeled. But the first step is to see it as non-negotiable. An absolute that never changes. You see, the biggest problem comes when we don't see life through a divinely focused lens. Yes, I admit, it is hard to write this book without referring explicitly to my Christian faith. If your mind-set is secular, I'm going to sound like a dinosaur to you. But if you humor me and consider some of my views, you might be surprised and find that there is something intriguing about how God's word gives us a clear blueprint on marriage, family, and parenting, and it gave us that blueprint centuries before some of the craziness we currently face even surfaced. So what other reference point do we have except the one that's always been there? Take your power back. Break the generational curses that have been part of our past. And remember: *They may not always like you, but they will come to love you.*

This is what I signed up for.

I said earlier that parenting is one of my greatest joys. But I must admit that at times it can be one of my greatest pains. I owe you honesty here because so many inspirational books don't keep stuff gully. This is not *The Cosby Show.* It's not *Leave It to Beaver.* There are no commercial breaks. No reruns. No edits to splice the parts you like together. This is "Live from New York . . ." It's straight up, spontaneous, learn as you go. It has kept me up late many nights worried, afraid, trying to figure out how in the world I got here. Sometimes life writes its own script. But when I see the smile on my little boy's face after I come home from a long trip, when my daughter can't wait to show me her new cheerleading routine *(My wife is kinda like those crazy mamas I talked about earlier!)*, when my oldest daughter was in her debutante ball and I escorted her, when my oldest son said he wants a marriage like mine—even though Tammy isn't his biological mom—it's worth it! Those things make driving home from the studio every morning at 5 a.m. just to take them to school worth it. They make catching red-eye flights to get back in time for soccer games worth every sleepless night in an airport. And they make every trip up and down the highway just to check on my baby in college worth it. It can, and *will*, be full of embarrassments, disappointments, mistakes, fears, and letdowns. But a young man taught me a lesson I'll never forget.

My sister has a daughter who Tammy and I helped raise. She married a great young man who is in the Army Reserve. After a couple of years and a new baby, he was stationed in Korea. Monica, my niece, was devastated; she would have to move away from all that she's ever known. Mike, the young man, came over to say good-bye, and I noticed something about his attitude. He wasn't upset, he wasn't complaining, and he wasn't distraught about having to move to a foreign place. When I asked him why he wasn't upset about moving so far away for two years with a new baby and still a newlywed, he looked at me calmly and said, "Uncle, I knew what I was signing when I signed the papers. Most of my friends signed up for the reserve just to get a check, not thinking that they would ever be called on. But I read the whole contract. I understood that there was always the possibility that I would be called on for duty. I read, I understood, and I settled in my mind, that this is what I signed up for. Not just the checks, not just the great insurance, but also for the possibility of battle, the possibility of war. It's what I signed up for."

Being a parent is going to have its perks—Easter suits, Christmas plays, and such. But it also has unexpected teenage pregnancies, car accidents, school meetings, and maybe even drug rehab. And when life seems to bring a storm of challenges, just remember: The contract says, *in this world, you will have tribulation; but be of good cheer. I have overcome the world* (John 16:33).

You are a parent. You are a leader. You are created to do this. Not just in convenient times, but in storms, in trials, in peace and in war. This is what I signed up for. This is what you signed up for. Read the contract.

Chapter Twelve

I Believe: The Blueprint for Faith

When a builder receives blueprints from an architect, he assumes that the papers he holds result from the years of schooling necessary to give you the right to call yourself an architect. So the client should be guaranteed a building designed by an architect who has been through a system of training and accountability, which gives you an assurance that it won't fall after it's built. A blueprint put together by just anyone on the street—someone with no references, no experience, no architectural training—could not be trusted as a plan to build from. Builders trust that the blueprint they receive is the real deal—tested, proven, and true. And so do their clients.

Now, for centuries people have lived and died for something that they believed was proven to be true, something they believed even in the midst of the most horrible tragedies ever recorded. These men and women endured those tragedies because they had a personal role in the greatest love story ever told, the greatest epic of all time. They saw that story—that love story—as the blueprint for their lives. It came by way of a collection of writings from people who were challenged, tested, trained . . . *and even killed.* So when those writers left their former ways of life, they did so because they believed that the gospel is true, that the ultimate good news story is certified, and that the tomb was and remains empty.

Please join me as I journey through the core blueprint of our lives, our faith.

Let me just state that I am a believer. Period. I believe in a God who reveals Himself in three ways. I believe that everything physical and visible was first preceded by that which is spiritual and invisible. I believe in a sovereign plan for humanity. I believe in the inerrancy of Scripture, that the plan for us was thought out intelligently and didn't just come about by a random series of natural selections.

I don't believe in religion. Instead, I believe I am the product of a relationship with a God who offers unlimited grace through an intimate friendship with His son. I believe that religion is man's pursuit of God, but the faith I affirm tells the story of a God in pursuit of us. Again, I am a believer. And I know that we believers are coming closer and closer to extinction.

The definition of "Christian" is changing drastically today. Even now the word's meaning varies broadly depending on where in this country you live. Comedian Bill Maher would call me an idiot; biologist and atheist Richard Dawkins would say that I'm a danger to society. But in the end, I am a Christian, and we Christians are a group of misfits and outsiders who for centuries have seemed to survive for no logical or scientific reason. We are not the most famous or the most talented, nor are we the elite. Certainly not in the eyes of the world. But despite persecution from rulers committed to annihilating the church (except when they thought they could use her for their own gain), we have survived. And although we have been deeply wounded over the last several decades, we continue not only to have a voice but also to offer hope to a world that still seems to view us as misfits. I am, and will forever be, Christian.

I am a son of the African-American church. I am entangled in her life. The institution called the church strikes a chord deep within me. I've seen her speak to starvation and hopelessness on city streets; I've seen her mend relationships torn apart by issues of race and politics.

During our country's darkest moments, many men and women placed their lives on the line because they believed that the all-knowing and all-powerful God created them to be much more than slavery and segregation allowed. They had had their dignity and self-respect stripped away, and the black church played a critical role in the uprising that restored them. I grew up in her hallways. There I learned the power of her music and the healing that lies in her songs—songs that remind us that tough times don't last forever, but tough people do.

I grew up seeing the older ladies in the church shout for hours. And when we got home they'd whoop our behinds for sitting in the back of the church and talking while the pastor preached. I love the fellowship of the black church. The chicken dinners in the fellowship hall, vacation Bible school, the three o'clock service where they served those triangle tuna fish sandwiches and the punch made from lime sherbet and Sprite. And, of course, the church hats!

Lord, have I seen some hats! Some so big that you had to find another seat just to see the choir. And let's not even talk about the choir! If you've never had the opportunity to see a black church choir do its thing, especially back in the day, don't die until you do. Choreography, church robes with all the trimmings, and a choir director who performs like a drum major at a black college football game! The tambourine players would play so hard that sometimes it looked like a battle to see who would "kill the crowd." I owe so much to the church, to the African-

American church. I've seen drug addiction and sickness left on the altar of her sanctuary. When all other institutions and corporations folded and closed their doors, the church—God's church—has been the beacon of light for all who chose to heed her call.

Not only do I believe in the Word, I also believe in God's mouthpiece—the preacher. Whether it's Spurgeon or Billy Graham, D. L. Moody or C. L. Franklin, C. S. Lewis or Caesar Clark, Tony Evans or T. D. Jakes, Martin Luther or Martin Luther King Jr., I am a fan of the preacher who can rightly divine the word of God so that both the most educated and the most unlearned receive a true revelation from the Scriptures, one that embodies the richness of God's promises and plan for us. As imperfect as the preacher has been, and will always be, I believe in the office; and I believe it should always be occupied with caution and soberness.

God bless the faith, God bless His sanctuary, and God bless the feet of them who preach the Gospel!

As I share my heart for the church, I recognize many will see anything other than positive and uplifting statements as bashing the house of God and those who protect her gates. Now I am *not* a church basher, and I never will be. But still I am amazed that, even in my community, many refuse to discuss the things that have hurt us, that have held us back, that have enslaved generations. When we address police brutality, we aren't saying that law enforcement as a whole should be condemned and discarded. But individuals within law enforcement who continue to abuse their positions of power should be held accountable for their actions so that others will not suffer at their hands. And as things go for law enforcement, so they should go for the church. Earlier in the book when I discussed the inappropriate sexual contact that too many young boys experienced at the hands of church elders, I defended the institution by saying that we can't bring down the entire church because of the horrible actions of a few. But that doesn't mean we should sweep those behaviors under the "sanctified" rug. So follow me.

What I'd like to do in this chapter is attempt to vibe with those of you out there who might be ready to allow the church to rescue you in the same way it rescued me. I would like to show you a way that you can consider the church as a safe haven, a friend, a life preserver. And even more broadly than the institution of the church, I'd like to demonstrate to you the power of faith.

It takes a supernatural power to love people who have done wrong.

It also takes a supernatural power to find hope when your entire autobiography has been hopeless. But that is what faith can bring you—undying hope. When you try to use the physical realm to overcome your troubles, you inevitably fail. You're going to wind up always depressed, always oppressed, always frustrated, always angry. And you'll keep asking yourself, *Why am I not getting the most out of my life?* But that's because you're trying to live your life using just a tiny part of your powers, with such a limited view of the things that are happening to you. Behind every physical act we see, behind every visible thing we perceive, there is a spiritual realm that has a strength and power that can't be conquered within our physical being. So you can't overcome your depression and anger with physical strength because those are not physical battles. They are supernatural battles. Once you enter the realm of faith, you start seeing things you never saw before, you start understanding the direction your life is taking.

It reminds me of what I went through one time when I was stuck on a plane that got delayed on the ground before take-off. I was stuck on this plane for five hours! And they were not letting us off. The toilets got stinky—everything got stinky! We were delayed so long that I called my dude in New Jersey (we were in Dallas) and asked him what was going on with the weather up north. I thought it must have been a typhoon or something up there and that the concert I was going to would be canceled or postponed. He said, "It's cloudy but that's about it." After a couple of hours, the pilot came on the microphone and told us about a major storm that was coming in. But the storm wasn't in Jersey; it was coming in from some other place, and that's what was causing the backup. My problem was I was calling somebody on the ground, my homeboy in Jersey, and his view was limited. He couldn't see what was going on from the ground. But when I was able to get information from somebody with a perspective that was much higher, he was able to tell me what was really happening. In other words, if we take off now, we could run into this other plane. So we needed to be right where we were, waiting on that runway. Think about how this applies to your own life. There may have been times when you had some delays in your life. It wasn't God saying, "No." It was God saying, "Not yet. Because if I do this for you now, then you might mess around and have a crash. Somebody else's life may be taking off now; there's enough room up here for both of you if you don't give up."

So if you don't see your life through a spiritual lens, you're going to be like me on that plane—frustrated and wondering, *Why am I not taking off? Why is my life not taking off? And why am I stuck in a stinky situation?* So you have to be in partnership with somebody who sits in another seat. Otherwise you will get on the phone and call people and talk to all these people who are on the ground like you and they're like, *I don't know; it's fine over here.* When you tap into somebody who is guiding the planes, they can say, *I got you. This is bad right now, but I've got a greater plan for you. Not only am I preparing it for you, I'm preparing you for it.*

That's why a spiritual life and a relationship with Christ are so important; it puts the bad, the uglies, the delays, in a different perspective. We get knowledge from someone who knows, instead of from people like you and me whose views are limited because we're all stuck on the ground.

Faith offers help in resisting temptation.

When you find yourself struggling with the flesh, faith provides us with another way of thinking about lust. That woman you're chasing over there is God's creation; that's God's daughter. So the things you choose to do *with* her and *to* her affect not only her but they affect your relationship with someone who is so much bigger than you. Someone who isn't scared when you cuss Him out; someone who sees everything you do. This isn't about making you live in fear, but there needs to be an accountability attached to your actions. And you need to have a spiritual understanding of soul ties, which I talked about in an earlier chapter.

When you see everything through the lens of God, you see that God has a purpose for your relationships that is more than just sex. When you lie with a woman, you're lying with her essence, her spirit. So you might think you're doing your thing, getting up and then leaving, but you're taking a sense of her with you. You take that into every relationship you have and you start adding all of those on top of one another. So when you succumb to these desires, understand that there's a price to pay. And as a married man, not only do I hurt God when I sin and mess around with another woman, I have also hurt him because I've hurt his daughter—my wife. He loves my wife just as much as he loves me. When you consider it that way, I think that changes your view of your actions. That gives you another layer you have to go through. You still with me?

We have to stop looking at sin in this fatalistic God-is-going-to-kill-you kind of way. No, it's deeper than that. It hurts God's heart to know that you would do that to his daughter. No man with any common sense would call a woman a "b*tch" in front of her daddy. No man with any common sense would put his hands on a woman while her daddy is sitting there. So if we can see women as daughters of this God that sees us as his sons, then you know God has seen me do this to his daughter, and that hurts him and disrespects him.

This message gets lost on a lot of powerful men in our society—even men in the pulpit. I think that's because once the floodgates of power and money are opened, it is natural for people—especially those of the opposite sex—to be attracted to anyone with the power and money. Being a church musician most of my life and leading choirs, I can guarantee you that most of the sexual experiences in my younger life came not because I was hot or my swag was on a hundred, thousand, or trillion. Matter of fact, I was pretty swagless. But I had a position of power. I was with women who on a normal day would never want to be with a little dude like me. I've seen with my own eyes, through my own experiences, the power of power.

I don't think we will ever fully understand the effect we have on mainstream society when they hear about Christian leaders falling into sexual sin. I must be *very* careful here because no one, especially me, can ever afford to be too confident that he or she will never fall. I hurt for ministries ruined because of sex. And only by the grace of God have I not been destroyed by the skeletons of my past. I cannot tell you how badly I sought help as a young man in the church struggling with sex. It was hard to find men who didn't see it as a "man's thing." And as a kid, I saw many men in and out of the church have extramarital relationships.

It happens so much today that when people in the church hear about a church leader fall, it's the talk one day but forgotten news the next. The leader is not held accountable. No one sits him down so he can be restored and the sickness *not* passed on to other men who follow him. When our spiritual leaders go through divorce, it sends the message that marriage is no longer a relevant institution in the twenty-first century. So the sheep go from marriage to marriage because the leaders set the stage.

A pastor once told me, "God didn't get angry at David for having an affair with Bathsheba; He was angry at David for killing her husband, Uriah." "God understands," he told me, "that men will have other sexual relationships." Can you believe this guy? This was a pastor, a man who supposedly led people in the ways of God. And he was giving me corrupt information that could have destroyed my life. Until the issue of sexuality is taken seriously by men and women in the faith, we will never heal correctly and our witness to the world will continue to be shaken. We will no longer be the standard but the joke.

I write passionately about the topic of faith because this is who I am. This is my home. It is in my DNA. I exist and live for the Christian faith. I am a better father because of it; a more sober husband because of its truth; a stronger man because of models of manhood in the Christian men I now serve and follow. Because of this truth, I am not in prison, not on drugs, not dying. So I beg you to listen.

Faith can help us be better people.

This is what it's all about, isn't it? How we can truly make a difference while we're here on this blessed soil. Sometimes I reflect on the faith chapter in Hebrews and I am blown away by the message. This chapter is so crazy to me! Paul starts naming names, going through this whole list of biblical heroes, Abraham, Sarah, Moses, telling us they all did this by faith. Then he says since we are surrounded by such a great crowd of witnesses, all these people before you have gone through what you've been through and now they are watching you and cheering for you. Crazy!

> Therefore, since we are surrounded by so great a cloud of witnesses, let us also lay aside every weight and the sin that clings so closely, and let us run with perseverance the race that is set before us, looking to Jesus the pioneer and perfecter of our faith, who for the sake of the joy that was set before him endured the cross, disregarding its shame, and has taken his seat at the right hand of the throne of God. Consider him who endured such hostility against himself from sinners, so that you may not grow weary or lose heart. In your struggle against sin you have not yet resisted to the point of shedding your blood. And you have forgotten the exhortation that addresses you as children—"My child, do not regard lightly the discipline of the Lord, or lose heart when you are punished by him; for the Lord disciplines those whom he loves, and chastises every child whom he accepts."
>
> Endure trials for the sake of discipline. God is treating you as children; for what child is there whom a parent does not discipline? (Hebrews 12:1–7)

The big homie Paul is saying there is this heavenly team of saints telling you that you can do it. Yes, you can get up and go to that job because people before you, in biblical times and in our times, took beatings and got sprayed by water hoses and got bitten in the butt by dogs, all so you could go to that job. And your hero Christ was even louder with it—he hung on the cross for your behind, so you better get up and live your life because heaven is full of winners cheering for you, believing in you. Let's go! The problem is, you have a lot of folks who wake up and nobody applauds them and nobody encourages them. Nobody is cheering them on and making them believe that their minimum wage job has any value. But heaven is saying every morning that you can do it today. You have all of heaven standing behind you, a cloud of people who have paved the way.

We need to realize that the spiritual component is the core of everything that is happening in our lives. As people of faith, as children of God, we trust and we believe that even the bad, the ugly, and the horrible God has allowed and He uses it for greater character development, greater strength, and greater maturity. That ticks a lot of people off. The question is always, *If God is so good, why does He let bad things happen?* That sounds like when our children say, If you really love me, why won't you let me have everything in the mall, why won't you let me stay out later, why won't you let me eat anything I want? Why do you give me all these rules and say "no" to all these things? But if parents can understand that the motive behind "no" is nothing but love and protection, why can't we understand the same thing with the heavenly Father? We understand that standard for parents, but as human children we don't seem to understand that standard for the heavenly Father. He is trying to make us more like Him. God is not as concerned about making us happy as making us His. It's just like the football coach. He's not trying to make his star quarterback feel good, he's trying to make the star quarterback a winner. Making us happy and feel good are by-products, not the foundation of anything we do. If we wait until we're happy, we'll never be motivated to do anything.

So this gets us into the area of prayer and the things we ask God to do for us. Most of our prayers, most of my prayer, most human prayer, at the forefront is always going to be seasoned and flavored with selfishness. We talk a lot in this book about selfishness because most of what we do as humans is self-serving. Our prayers are self-serving because we've become misguided in what faith is really about. Faith is not about trying to give us our best life now. You can just read self-help books if you want an instant, microwaveable me. But God is not in the business of microwaveable me's. He's not trying to create a disposable you. He's trying to create a you who can last through the storms and tests and trials, through situations and calamities and horrors and disappointments. He's trying to mold us into people of weight, people with depth, people with roots. He's trying to have our roots go deep. Trees that last through the storm are the older trees that have roots that have gone deep into the soil over the years. *Make me happy . . . Give me a raise . . . Make me pretty and successful*—those are not deep roots or deep prayers. Most of us, if we're being honest, have to admit we don't really know how to pray. I have to work on this every day myself. But that's what's so cool about God: He's committed to the whole journey. God is down for the long run, for me to learn it over time as long as I'm committed to the classroom. He's committed to the process, no matter how long it takes me. Our prayers always include *our* wishes and desires. There's nothing wrong with our wishes and desires, but prayers also have to include not *my* will but *Thy* will be done. You might be praying for a raise, but what if God wants you to have challenge and conflict because God knows in another year He has a better job with a higher position where you need to be even stronger? You may be praying to keep a job, but God needs you to go through this fight and conflict with your boss who's driving you crazy because the next boss will be even harder. He knows if you don't learn to have the strength on this level, you won't be able to handle the pressure at the next level. That's why we always have to include *Thy will be done* in our prayers, not *my will*. His will is always better.

Get yourself to a house of worship.

> "There was the car wreck, and the bullet, and the doctor's diagnosis, and the pink slip at work—these were all things that God spared me from in the past week. Things I wasn't even aware of. And church is my time to go and be in His presence and thank Him. Even when there are sick, stupid people there who are just as broken as me, church service is my time to be reminded of how good He's been to me all through the week. Yes, there may have been some bad things that happened, but there were a lot of things that didn't happen, a lot more bad things that could have happened. So for that I'm going to show my appreciation." —Unknown

The value of being alive has to be greater to me than the value we put on having fun. After all, we find the time to do other things. It may be cold outside, but we'll go to the club. We find the time to get our hair done. We're supposed to be in a recession, but nobody is walking around here nappy-headed. We're still poppin' bottles at the club. We may have had to make up some things from leftovers and kind of recycle some joints, but we are still dressed and looking fresh. Nobody is walking around not fresh (translation: looking nice). See, it's easy for people to go to church when they're in a position of need because they're desperate. But when everything is gravy you don't think you need it. For example, after September 11 people were standing in line to go to church like it was an Uncle Luke concert back in the day. It was packed because people were desperate and afraid. But why do we have to wait for that? Why do we have to wait for moments of fear, worry, and trouble? To show love for somebody who loves you when there's no fear or trouble, who gives you oxygen when you wake up in the morning.

You could breathe when you woke up today, but we don't even say "thank you" sometimes. So the motivation is He gives me a billion times more in just one day than I could ever give him. One day! Can you believe that?

After Sundays, you grow and you may want to start going to one of the night services for Bible study, maybe be part of the men's or women's fellowship to try to go even deeper. Because church is really supposed to be a community for your spiritual development. We live in a world that sucks everything spiritual away from us. We work jobs that beat us down, life beats us down, our spouses beat us down, our careers beat us down, growing old beats us down. Church is a place that reminds you and lifts you up. But it's important to find a church community that fits—you shouldn't be there just because Big Mama went there and you were raised in that church. That doesn't mean anything. If you're not healthy and growing there, then it's time for you to bounce and find a place where you can be healthy and grow. You have to become part of the fabric of the church—that's when you grow, when you are in the fabric and not just on Sunday morning, trying to fit God in. God is my life and everything else fits in.

How to get past a lack of respect for the pastor.

The Bible challenges men to be wary of taking the leadership position in the church. The Bible says you should think twice and soberly about even thinking of taking that position, as if it's asking, *Are you sure you want this?* (James 3:1).

Your view of the pastor needs to change before he even has a chance to fall, before he can lose your respect. You have to be proactive instead of reactive about your view of the preacher. You have to go through that door realizing and remembering that he's just a man. So if and when he falls, he doesn't have far to go. He's a man who helps to present the meal, but he is never to be the meal. He's a chef, a servant, a cook, and I appreciate him for that and I pray for his health and his life.

But I also want to admit to men and women who are clergy that I don't fully understand the burden and responsibility of your position. And I never will. I'm not called to tell you how to do your job. But I *am* called to say what I see. I may not have credibility as a teacher, but I *do* as a student, especially as one seeking to live what you teach.

Every now and then you hear some of the older saints in the church say, "There was a time when the preacher would walk down the street and other men would take off their hats in honor of the man of God." Or someone else will talk about a time when, if you told someone you were a Christian, they would stop swearing (or, as I call it, cussin') or would feel uncomfortable having a drink around you because of the title you wore. Even those who didn't agree with your faith would respect your stand and even add some of your views on how to be good and moral to their lives. The person who held the faith once had some juice in society and politics, in television and music. Christian values were once seen in every area of life. But just like juice in a carton, if it just sits, never being used, it expires. The Christian whose life never becomes useful, who doesn't live for the purpose he was created for, or who uses his position in wrong ways, ends up being good for nothing. How can salt that loses its flavor ever become salty again?

Somewhere between the pastor becoming the local neighborhood hero and the church becoming the social hangout for a culture trying to find its voice, some folks lost their way, their vision, and their purpose.

I say *some*, not all, because there are great men and women in this country doing incredible work for the sake of the cross. Which makes it even more urgent that we cut down the weeds so that these individuals can be seen even more clearly by a society that is constantly changing what it believes, and what it believes in.

Every group in society struggles with power. Power is sexy. And it can be very addictive. You can change the course of people's lives if you are in a position of power. You can have a hand in negotiating what happens in society if you have access to power. The church and her community are in many respects no different from any other community in life. She is filled with humans, not gods. Flawed, imperfect humans who need to be fully aware at all times that, if left to their own understandings, they will waver through life with a standard that's constantly changing. Some churches and church leaders have also had a role in misusing power in the name of God.

Racism could never have survived if the church had called it sin. Instead, many churches and slave owners misinterpreted the Scriptures to benefit their wicked hearts. And some pastors in the South even spoke from the pulpit to challenge those who desired their freedom to deny the temptation from Satan and see their situation—their *slavery*—as a service to God. Stupid. This is still an issue, and it *must* be dealt with, but not by opportunists looking to continue the great divide that we see during our "segregated Sundays."

That thirst for power has caused some in the faith to build small kingdoms. And with any kingdom, there must be a king. The people watch as the kingdom begins to benefit no one but the king. And the church becomes a place where we no longer show up to serve but to be served. The older members make the younger ones feel like outsiders, so the young are not motivated to be part of the body. You even hear folks say things like "this is *my* church" and "*we* don't do that here," so you feel like you don't belong unless you're part of the "club."

And leaders desire a higher platform and better title. The

sheep watch as the pastor changes titles, seeks more space for a bigger sanctuary, and buys time on Christian television. And the kingdom, along with the *human* king, becomes bigger and bigger. Please note that there is nothing wrong with any of these things by themselves. But if the king no longer has a heart to serve, and to be seen serving, how will the sheep ever learn service?

It is easy to pursue power and miss His presence. So the sheep lose their way and develop the desires they see in the king. They begin to want their own kingdoms. Look at the history of denominations and you'll see the pattern. Everyone desires his or her own kingdom. And because this flesh never gets satisfied, the cycle never ends. So no one learns that "the first shall be last" because the desire is to be first and the goal is "me." I am not, as some would argue, calling for poverty. I am pointing out how dangerous power can be. Whether we're talking platforms or positions, the church is not ours, heaven is not ours, and the Christian faith is not ours. It belongs not only to the powerful but even more to the weak. And when we abuse a church platform that was originally intended to serve from, we contaminate it and forget that we are *wanted but not needed*.

The natural partner of power is, and will always be, money. From small neighborhood churches to mega-churches, throughout the history of the modern church, we have struggled with the issue of money. The local pastor in the seventies had a Cadillac as big as the local pimp's. But the payment fell on the shoulders of his small congregation. Jim and Tammy Bakker gave the country a firsthand view of the unraveling of a multimillion-dollar empire filled with all the trappings—and *traps*—of greed and materialism. Money has brought down some of our best and brightest. And it has revealed some of the worst wolves in sheep coats with mink trim.

In the last few decades the paradigm changed from practical

theology to prosperity. Many preached that, "if you are a child of God, you need to drive this, and God wants you to have a house like that." "Name it and claim it" was the hustle, and everybody jumped on board. Even at gospel concerts, if you didn't repeat the well-known clichés of the time, people wouldn't get excited. If you don't know them, let me share some: "Touch your neighbor and tell 'em, 'Your blessing is on the way!'" or "Reach up and grab it!" or my all-time favorite "Money cometh!" People believed that if they just gave a little more, a pie-in-the-sky blessing would set them on the path to having a car like the pastor's and living in a house like the pastor's. Because the pastor said it and he has it; so I want it, too. And they bought houses they couldn't afford, cars they couldn't afford, got credit and loans they couldn't afford, because some preacher misused the Scripture that says "the wealth of the wicked is stored up for the righteous."

And then . . . the recession.

People started losing the homes they couldn't afford. The prophecy didn't come to pass. The good life never came. And people stopped writing "money cometh" on their dollar bills and began to ask, "What happened?"

Let me say that I am not against prosperity; I am against prosperity theology. A method of teaching that says, "God doesn't want you to be broke, God wants you to have what the world has since your Father owns cattle on a thousand hills." God *never* promised that. God didn't even promise that to His own son. Jesus' package included a cross.

So people now feel lied to. We told them the blessing was coming. We told them they deserve that house, so they went out and got it. Even if they couldn't afford it, because it is human nature to want the benefits of a relationship but not the difficult, hard stuff. Many people leaned to what was more attractive. But when the bottom fell out of the market, and people started to lose their jobs, they struggled. Because some of their leaders fed them "junk food" instead of substance. If a sermon about prosperity preached in Kansas can't be preached in Kenya, it's not the Bible's definition of prosperity. If we had fed them the stuff nobody likes, like "in this world you will have tribulation" or "you are strangers and aliens here; this isn't home" or "count it all joy," we would have been in line with the Bible. These truths may not always be sexy to the flesh, but they don't let people down when the storm comes. Basically, it isn't *either/or* but *both/and*: Storms will come as surely as good times.

Let me share with you that I have run into several people, good people, who say, "God's people are recession-proof. We're on God's economy." Do you know how dangerous it is to tell people that? They go and continue to spend, not being wise, because some preacher told his sheep they are recession-proof. A Christian is not recession-proof, bulletproof, or AIDS-proof. As long as you live, when it rains in your city, your house gets wet, too. So how we've talked about and dealt with money has been one of the most damaging things to our witness to the world. And last, if we never see our leaders content, how will we learn to be content?

Let's make those who lead give an account.

A leader who has no accountability is a wreck waiting to happen. Every doctor who opens a practice, prescribes medication, or performs procedures must be board certified. He must have a group of other doctors and medical professionals he answers to. And that group doesn't allow him to make medical decisions without accountability. As we have seen in Michael Jackson's case, a doctor left to himself—without accountability—is dangerous and a potential murderer. But if the doctor has the correct type of accountability and legal covering, the patient has the assurance that the doctor is qualified for the job.

A church is one of the few businesses you can open in this country without committee oversight, without board certification, and in some cases even without a business permit. Some people have even turned their homes into churches. A person can start a Bible study on a whim with no okay from any supervising leadership. That can be very dangerous. Just as you wouldn't go to a doctor who has no license, you shouldn't sit under a church leader with no covering. He's doing surgery on people's souls with no accountability.

And millions of Americans are walking around with botched surgery on their lives because they took seriously the medicine "God's doctor" prescribed for them. You wouldn't do that to your body; you shouldn't do that to your soul. Because of the seriousness of your spiritual well-being, who you trust with the health of your soul is a very serious thing. You should choose someone on the basis of the health of that person's soul. You owe it to yourself to choose a spiritual physician who is board certified.

A special Word for men.

To my brothers, let me say that I understand why there aren't more of us in the pews on a Sunday morn. We aren't there because we're not celebrated to be there; we're not encouraged to be there. We don't see a place for ourselves there. We may not be emotional, we may not be as expressive, so when you have churches that are built on those themes, we don't find a place. For example, the church I attend in Texas has a strong presence of men. That's because our pastor is a man's man. He likes football. He's not always running around just surrounded by women, with all these female assistants and workers. His sermons are very masculine; the men feel like they have a place.

The church has to make men feel like they are important and welcome there. That's the only way you are going to get men back to the church. What women have to do is they have to stop bringing the pastor home—"Pastor said this . . . Pastor said that . . ." A man doesn't want another man up in his house all the time. The woman has to say to her man, "I would love for you to come with me and I believe in the man you want to be for our family." When a woman reminds a man of his role and position and reminds him of his importance, that's when he will take that chance and go. And if the church reinforces what she says, then you have a man who's willing to try. So the pastor and the women have to work together to reinforce. Instead of, "You should have heard what the pastor said today. . . . You should have been there." No, you leave all of that outside the door. Otherwise, that man is going to be thinking, "Did the pastor say anything about you gossiping all day? . . . Did he say anything about you being on the phone all day? . . . You laying hands on people at the church, well come lay some hands on me!" If your husband's not seeing the Gospel make you any different, make you a better person, what's going to be his motivation to go? A lot of women have used the church and the Gospel to make themselves bigger than their husbands, to attack their husbands. And too many pastors have encouraged that instead of trying to tear it down. Dudes love community. That pastor has to make himself accessible to those dudes. He has to come around and say, "Hey, wassup, fellas! What's going on with y'all boys? You know what? On Saturday morning let's do breakfast. Let's chop." You have to do that with dudes. If you're the pastor and you're not spending time with your dudes, that's real weak.

We may not like veggies, but we need them.

In a time of blitz marketing, faster communication, and attention-deficit disorder, it is easy for church to become an always camera-ready production. So we lose our authenticity and our absolutes; we give people "Jesus lite" to keep them coming back to the show. It's no longer just Jesus, it's "Jesus and . . ." We embrace anything that doesn't alienate. You wouldn't do that in your relationship with your significant other. You wouldn't be pluralistic with someone you're in love with. If that person is with you, neither of you can have somebody else you go home to. You force each other to make a choice: "Either them or me," you say. But when we tell people Christ requires the same commitment, we are attacked and labeled as self-righteous and judgmental. Now, I'm not the smartest dude in the world, so if it's simple to me, it should be simple to anyone. If Jesus is not who he says he is, he's a liar. Period. Not he *may* be who he says he is; not just a good guy. Liars are *not* good guys.

We can't be afraid to preach a truth that may cause the crowd to walk away. We can't be so concerned about staying relevant that we are no longer different. While seeking to be progressive, we cannot cease to be authentic. And there is a way to do it without coming across like June and Ward Cleaver. I love style. I dig flair and visions that are fresh and banging. But when it comes to the message that saved me and many like me, I'll act a fool to defend it.

And I don't grow from a message that just tells me what feels good and lets me do whatever I want to. If that were the case, open up the bar, turn on the music, and bring on the females. Because that would make more sense. But we need vegetables, even if we don't always like them. We need to know that God isn't a punk who just sits around waiting for you to pull Him out like a spare tire. He is a God who hates racism. He despises people who think they've got it all together. He's not an excuse for a family reunion. And He refuses to be a sugar daddy, a "Santa Claus"–like genie who fulfills all your heart's desires. He is the God who calls you to choose. Just like you called the one you love to do the same.

I dream of a day when churches in our country have a series of Sundays when white, black, and Hispanic pastors switch pulpits with each other and share how each community feels about the most segregated day of the week; when the members are forced to feel uncomfortable until the issue is truly dealt with; when true love and trust are established in the house of God.

I dream of a day when men in positions of power are not afraid to hold their colleagues accountable for the messages they preach and the lives they live. I know there will never be a perfect individual. But at least many hands will be there to try to catch him before he falls.

I dream of a day when our passions move past topics that are convenient and force us into areas that get our hands dirty; when we clean the dirt under our own beds before we try to clean the world. Gay rights and unborn babies are not the only things evangelicals should shout about. How about jealousy? Greed? Hypocrisy? Adultery? And so on. Even if they do hit too close to home.

I dream of a day when the world once again respects what it sees of us. Not for the words that come out of our mouths, but for our lives that speak louder than any sermon. A day when we are willing to stand for something, rather than to fall for anything. They may never agree with our message, but they will have to admire the changes they see in our lives—the commitment to our spouses, the investment in our children, and our pledge to the faith.

Another man had a dream once; I hope I don't have to die to see mine.

Every man that has impacted my life has been a preacher. My mom told me that when I was four, I said I wanted to be like

Martin Luther King. I adored preachers as a kid. How they moved a crowd. How they spoke with such authority. And how sharp they were on Sunday morning. I embraced the good and struggled with the bad. But I am still a fan, a product of the preacher, the man of God. I need you; we need you. We don't want to make the same mistakes as those who came before (and of some still around today). We want to be smarter, to learn more, to have self-control, and to have healthy, happy homes.

Teach us that no one should call himself a preacher without counting the cost!

Teach us that your most vulnerable time is when you just left the pulpit and are empty, for that is the easiest time to fall into sexual sin!

Teach us that you never counsel women by yourself!

Teach us that your secretary cannot be prettier than your wife!

Teach us that money is not evil, but the love of it is!

Teach us how to tell the people that we walk through some of the difficult issues of the day and that we don't have all the answers!

Teach us how to ask for help before it's too late!

Please, teach us! Show us your scars. Share with us your failures. Give us lessons from your mistakes. You are the teacher. We are the pupils. Whatever you teach us, good or bad, we *will* learn.

Chapter Thirteen

THE BLUEPRINT FOR MOVING FORWARD

So here we are. After all the delays, changes in plans, the firing and rehiring of crews, applying for permits, and, of course, rethinking the blueprint, we are at the end. You now have materials and tools that can stand the test of time. Yes, there were challenges, disappointments, and there will be more, but we never give up. We've torn down old walls, full of decay and mildew, and replaced them with new and stronger ones. In the past, we would have just patched up a hole here and there. But all that did was leave you frustrated. This new blueprint calls for changes—changes in the way you think, the way you love, *what* you love, your character and values.

You've been at the old place long enough. You've cried and cursed at the same stuff long enough. You've played the blame game with everybody from Grandma Myrtle to Uncle Cleophus far too long. With nothing else to prove, it's time to pack the bags, fill out the change of address card, enroll the kids in the new school, welcome new friends, *and move*. Although the new you will need touching up from time to time, your new building and new life await you. The keys have been delivered, old habits have been addressed. We've taken hard looks in the mirror, we've admitted our own roles in some of the bad things that have happened in our lives. We've realized that—no matter how old we are, no matter how much stuff we've picked up along the way—it's never too late to start again.

With the new pages of your life written in the ink of His love and commitment, you have the potential for greatness. And you can help those around you become great, too. Because, remember, *it's not all about you.*

No matter the mistakes of other builders, for you it's a new day! As a reminder, just in case you've forgotten, let's review some of the highlights one more time. We talked about issues from sex to the soul and discussed commitments ranging from faith to family. We talked about the fact that relationships are not microwaveable, that they take time and engagement. We discussed our roles as parents, how our children don't raise themselves, how the job of churches and schools is to come alongside the home but never to take the place of the home.

We talked about man's need for woman's unconditional love, that each man needs a woman to love him for the man he almost is, and for the man he wants to be. We talked about how men on one level or another will always have to be wary of the penis problem, how we can never let our desires determine our future. We talked about a woman's worth, about how she can control the environment simply by how she introduces herself to us—whether she introduces herself as the woman who talks with her body or the one who remembers the value of her body. Either way, we respond to the one we are introduced to.

We discussed intimacy, the capacity to be real with another person. Sex before marriage was likened to the trailer to a movie. It only shows you the exciting parts to get you to buy a ticket. But the movie is never as good as the commercial. We also talked about the faith, the church, and the job of her people. If you preach to people without loving them, then you've wasted your time; going to church no more makes you a Christian than being in a garage makes you a car. We even tried to discuss the elephant in the room—racism. Generation begets generation in a never-ending cycle of hate. It falls to this new generation to make the difference. But until we do, no more sweeping under the carpet; instead, we need to take a good look at the man or woman in the mirror. And finally, one of my favorites is gardening or, as I put it, lifescaping. We saw that you have to deal with the weeds in your life; whether those weeds are attitudes, a mind-set, or people—whatever sprouts up in your way chokes out real life and keeps real joy from growing—the change you desire can never happen until you are bold enough to chop down the weeds you face. If I don't deal with them, my biggest enemy will always be "inner me."

So now it's time to move. From who you were, who they said you were, even who you thought you were, to the man or woman with a new plan, a divine plan. If I could use something a little more specific to my faith, a plan that was created before the beginning of time. *(You know I gotta show love to my Hero every chance I get!)* A plan not only created for you before you first cried in the delivery room, but a plan custom-made just for you. No one else can accomplish and achieve what you were put here to do. You've wasted too much time already trying to be like others, trying to be like the pompous, pious people at church because that's what you thought loving God looked like. No, it just looks like you—tattoos, nose pierced, criminal record, long dreadlocks, whatever *you* look like! A path has been charted for you to travel, and the guy in the Armani suit can't wear your skinny jeans; they don't fit! There is a couture plan tailored specifically for you. But you have to . . .

Follow the director.

After Michael Jackson died, the director of the "Billie Jean" video was on TV talking about the making of that historic video. He said that because the King of Pop was such a great spontaneous dancer, he had to make sure that Michael understood to step on certain steps because they had been pre-lit. Every spot where Michael stepped would light up whenever he moved there. If Michael had felt like doing his own thing and chose to step on other spots, he would have found himself dancing in the dark (which might have been cool for Bruce Springsteen but would have ruined "Billie Jean"!) because the spots wouldn't have been pre-lit. But as long as Mike followed the director's instructions and stepped in the prearranged spots, every move he made would light up. The right spots had been planned to light up for him long before he started dancing.

God has gone ahead of you and prearranged your steps; He was your director before you even started shooting, moving ahead of you and prelighting your way. He has already chosen the stage. The track has already been laid out by the hottest producer on the planet—or should I say, of the planet. He has a plan just for you, and if you follow His direction, your steps will light up!

Our problem is that we want to go in on our own—with our own goals, our own melodies, our own lyrics, our own agendas, our own ways of doing business—and do it our way. Then we get upset when the lights don't come on. We want the security of having a director on the set, but we also want to tell him what steps to light up. So we end up living life stepping on the wrong spots. And no matter how hard we try, they just won't light up. But what's the use of God being there if we don't let Him do His thing?

You didn't come this far, struggle this long, and hurt this much just to go through life stumbling over steps, trying to figure out what path to take or which spots to hit. And you certainly don't want to keep covering the same ground, tracing and retracing your steps because you weren't quite sure which fork to follow or turn to make. You and I are not equipped to direct ourselves. We simply aren't that good at it. Sorry.

There, I said it! That admission alone seems so un-American because we are taught that we can do anything. But this is not about being a strong citizen. It's about hitting the right steps so that your way lights up as you go. Not living behind a question mark. Not always wondering whether you should have married someone else, whether you should have taken that job transfer, or whether you should have shown a little more leg to get that part in the movie. Not living in a world of maybes and shouldas— "maybe I shoulda done this . . . maybe I shoulda done that. . . ." That can drive somebody crazy!

You don't get dropped off after birth and then have to find your own way home. It doesn't work like that. You're equipped with a navigational system that can take you from wherever you are and reroute you home. You're too valuable to God to be left to figure out this thing called life all by yourself.

I'm glad Michael listened to the director. "Billie Jean" is one of my favorite videos. As soon as you hear the base line (doom do doom da doom doom doom doom), you know it's about to go down! The socks, the curl that needs to be freshened up just a bit—it's the best video ever. It would have been awkward watching him stumble all over the place, sometimes in the light, other times in the dark, some squares lighting up, some just staring back at him. He's a great dancer. But he's at his best when he follows the right direction.

A painful good-bye.

So as you close one door to open another, there's always a last-minute dilemma to deal with. As you prepare to move to the "new" you, you have to go through the painful process of deciding what stays, what goes. Some of us are packrats. We hold on to every piece of junk, afraid to let it go for various reasons. But in this new space of your life, you don't have enough room for unnecessary things. So now you have to spend a whole week-end—or a whole "season"—going through the painful process of saying good-bye to them, so that you can say hello to all the things you're about to gain.

My man Paul had to do that in the Bible. Around AD 62, he wrote to the church in a town called Philippi, telling them how he took care of his business before becoming a Jesus follower. He told the church that he was the guy people used to call if they wanted to make one of these people called Christians come up "missing"; he was *the* guy for that job. Well educated, from a popular family, with all the love he got from the streets, he was the original "shot caller." But after a life-changing event that brought him down to his knees, he ended up becoming part of the crew he had become famous for killing. Now looking back over his life, his accomplishments, his former career achievements, he says, while writing behind bars in a dark, lonely cell, *Because of what I have gained now having Christ as my Lord, I consider everything else in my past as garbage, and suffer losing everything that meant something to me, so that I may find Him* (Philippians 3:8).

That's fire right there!

Could it possibly be that the pain we as people have gone through over the last few years is part of the painful process of saying good-bye to things that mattered too much, things that have become too important, things that were never meant to be your "source" but just your "resource"? See, your job is not your source, it's just your resource. Friends, talents, whatever, if you put them in the category of source, you give them too much power; when they fail, you fail with them. So God at times has to shake things up in life to remind us never to put things in the wrong place. GM, Ford, banks, they are not your source. God is your source. So if those other things close down, you don't have to lose your mind or live in a funk because your source can always create another resource. (I feel like preaching as I write this at three in the morning!)

I believe that's why Paul said he had to "suffer losing everything for the sake of gaining Christ"; the process of giving up in order to gain, of saying good-bye in order to say hello can be painful.

What if the stuff you know—the stuff you've come to love— won't fit in the new space? It has sentimental value like an old couch that's torn and has thick gray tape holding the armrest together; it's ugly, but it's all you've ever had. Or it may be a person who isn't good for you, but your emotions make it hard to let go.

"That I may gain."

Remember what my boy Paul said? He said, "I lose *that I may gain*."

It's easy to let go of a hooptie if you know that the new S class is in your driveway. It's a lot less painful to let go of the boyfriend who sleeps all day when you know that Mr. Tall, Dark, Abs with Benefits is right around the corner.

While going through the pain of letting go, you should never forget what waits for you at your new location, in your new season, in your new place of grace and wholeness. Most people grow frustrated because they lose sight of that truth. When you lose focus on what you're building, or even rebuilding, you lose your smile, you lose your peace, and ultimately you lose your purpose.

One year after Hurricane Katrina, I was pleased to go to New Orleans for a concert. While I was there, I filmed my own little documentary in the communities that still were not rebuilt. In one of the hardest hit areas, people were still living in FEMA trailers parked right in front of their damaged homes. You could feel the frustration of the community as we drove down the street and stopped to talk to people. You see, the trailers were not built to be lived in that long. They were only meant for temporary occupancy. Because time had passed and people were still waiting for their homes to be rebuilt, the cramped living conditions just fueled the frustration over the unfinished business in the community.

However, we noticed one guy who was different from everyone else. For while everyone else's trailer faced the street, he had the city turn his trailer around to face his house as it was being rebuilt. So every morning when he left to go to work, the first thing he saw that day was his permanent address—even though he was still living in a temporary trailer. No, there was not a lot of work going on at his house, but each brick got him closer to leaving the trailer. He was able to keep his joy because he never took his eyes off what he was going to gain, so his current situation never got in the way of what he was looking forward to.

Paul knew what he was gaining and never took his eyes off that truth. Even though he was beaten, laughed at, and left to die, he simply considered all that just a bad day when compared to what he knew was coming. I promise you, he's a better man than me! His kept his eye on the goal line by letting go of things he once valued greatly. He was willing to give up one thing to receive another thing so much better. How can God put in your hands what He has for you if your hands are already full? For all that Paul lost, he was only able to write the stuff he did because the old stuff couldn't even compare to the new.

You still with me?

After back and forth discussions for several years, my wife hung my album plaques in the house. Now I am grateful for the lives that my work has touched, but I've always struggled with the trophies and images because, from time to time, I made "little gods" out of them.

One night while reading the passage from Philippians, I happened to look at those plaques and had an "aha" moment. My heart realized that all the things I valued—all the things that gave me my identity and status once upon a time—can't compare to the love and relationship I'm developing with my Father in heaven. But the process of getting to the point of being able to say that has been painful, sometimes *very* painful. Some albums didn't sell, some tours were canceled, some relationships with friends or coworkers ended sourly. But all those things were part of the plan, and they helped me learn what was, and *is*, my source. I've lost a lot, but man, I've gained so much more!

What stays, and what goes?

As you begin to move from where you are to where you're going, things can look pretty scary. Despite the commercials, the future doesn't come with an "easy" button, and success isn't guaranteed. Trying to figure out which relationships can stay and which need to go isn't the easiest thing, especially if some of the ones that need to go have been in place for years. Emotionally, soul ties sink deep roots into the soil of your heart. As you become a more mature, healthier you, it's in your best interest to take inventory of the things and people around you, just to be sure that they belong in the "new you" you're building.

Plants (and other living things) may do well in certain climates but die in other ones. Once, when watching an awards show with a prominent music executive, I saw an urban artist win for his category; when he came onstage to accept the award, his whole neighborhood seemed to come with him. Now, it was obvious that most of these people hadn't written any songs, played any instruments, or balanced any financial books. But since they were the artist's homies, they came onstage to get some love. I'll never forget this wise man sitting next to me, who had years of experience with this kind of music, say, "Kirk, remember one thing, you can't take the hood with you." He was right:

Everybody you know can't always go.

It's the same with seasons in your life. The person who fit in well during one season may not fit well—may even be a fatal distraction—in the new one. And just because you know them, grew up with them, or had children with them doesn't mean they should automatically get a free trip with you to your new destination in life.

So how do we figure this out? As we unpack our lives and move from one place in life to the next, how do we tell our hearts who and what stays, who and what goes?

Deposits and withdrawals.

Here the key is to see your life, your soul, as an account. For some of us, our real bank accounts may make this illustration a little scary, but hang in there with me. If you're in a relationship, a friendship, a job, or even close to family members who are nurturing, giving, always inspiring you to do better, to finish your degree, to take that trip, or whatever the case, they're making deposits into your life. They're adding something that creates wealth inside you. Those deposits end up filling your account with peace, fulfillment, and all the other ingredients of a healthy individual.

But if your environment is always negative, discouraging, full of drama and weighing you down, those people are making withdrawals. They are not adding to your life; they are subtracting from it. And we all know what happens to any account that has more taken out of it than was put into it. You wake up one day and your self-esteem, your faith, your confidence, your trust—all these accounts have insufficient funds.

You know the takers. You don't have to be super-smart to know that something about this job or that person doesn't feel right, doesn't have the spirit of a win-win that will have all parties gaining from the relationship. Who calls more? Who stays later? Who compliments and supports more? If you see it and ignore it, don't blame the teller at the bank. Blame yourself!

So dig through the junk, do a balance sheet on your relationships, and see who makes you better, what completes you, as well as who takes more than they give, what environments leave you drained when you walk out the door to head back home. After you've done the balance sheet, ask God for the courage and strength to apply the lessons you've learned to build the new building, your new life, and truly trust in His unmerited favor. Like a mother with her child, guard and protect your emotional and spiritual accounts.

And make yourself a new budget. Cut out the fat and make sure you're making deposits into someone else's account. It helps with the selfish stuff we talked about earlier. And finally, keep your account full. You never know when you'll need that extra joy!

Even with a blueprint, directions, or a manual, no one is ever guaranteed smooth sailing through life without disappointments. Life is interesting, and we'll never fully understand it this side of Heaven. God doesn't always let us sneak a peak to see how the plot will play out; we may get glimpses of what we are becoming, but He never shows us the full trailer. That's why faith, believing what you can't see but know to be true, is more valuable than gold.

A young dude I mentor tells me that he gets discouraged feeling like the only person who still believes what God says about right and wrong. He says sometimes he wonders whether it's for nothing that he's tried to do things God's way. Especially with everybody bailing out and changing their stand.

I have to remind him, as I have to remind myself: If we come to the end of all this and find out we were wrong, what did we lose? Some parties? Some girls? Some money? Was paying for that family's dinner without them knowing going to be something we regret when we take our last breath? Was choosing the "narrow way" instead of those females at the club gonna make our home-going less meaningful? If we die and there's nothing there, who will be there to say, "I told you so"?

But dude, what if we're right? I believe in my heart that we're right, man! I believe that even though sometimes we look like we're losing, the battle is far from over. We can't walk out just because we don't like the part of the story we happen to be looking at now.

You ever been to the movies with your friends, y'all sitting there with your drinks and treats, excited about this movie you've been dying to see? Once it starts, it moves kinda slow. Then it picks up some. And you think it's turned for the better when all of a sudden it seems to get worse again. Frustrated, you leave your friends there to go home because you can't believe you spent your hard-earned money on this garbage.

By the time you get home, your friend calls to tell you that, as soon as you left, the monster came and ate the lady, and the people were running screaming because the monster stole their shoes and the world was about to be taken over by little green people with big apple heads! And everybody in the theater was crying because they thought they were about to die, and then the hero jumped on top of the monster with his tight "hero man" drawers on and killed the monster! Then he jumped in the monster's stomach and pulled the lady out, got everybody back their shoes and saved the world from the little midget green apple-headed people! They lived happily ever after. Man, you should have stayed; you missed the best part!

I'm sorry, that was fun. But the line to remember is, *"You should have stayed; you missed the best part!"*

People are leaving their faith, walking out on God too soon, before their lives get to the best part. They look at the housing market crash, the financial challenges in their lives, dreams that have yet to be filled, and because things are not going the way they planned, they think, "This is not the movie I paid to see." And because they feel robbed, they leave their families, attempt suicide, or simply stop living. Like a flower in the ground that's gone too long without water, they're still there, but all the beauty and life is gone.

I'm encouraging you to stick around a little bit longer. There's a part coming up that you're going to like. Yes, the scene you're in feels like it'll never end and the focus even seems a little blurry. But if you hang in there, ignoring the crying babies and the teenagers on their phones (which they were told to turn off!), there's something great coming up! So I'm asking, I'm begging you to stick around. Or you're gonna miss the best part! And, oh yeah! Some movies have to have a sequel, a part two. And if you think you've seen God do some great things, you ain't seen nothing yet!

"When do I see it, Kirk? When do I get out of this difficult place?"

May I suggest that when it seems to be getting harder, you might be closer than you realize? Growth is often defined by difficulty. Remember Kennedy's growing pains in her leg? The more difficult the math problem, the more advanced the course.

A few days ago, school started here in Texas. Kennedy came home complaining about the size of her books. Now in the third grade, she came home screaming about how hard the school year is going to be because the books are huge! But, I told her, they are supposed to get bigger when you go to another level.

That weight you feel is not a curse but rather a sign that you're going to the next level. And the bigger books show that you passed the last grade.

I believe. I *gotta* believe!

With all this hopelessness in the world, I gotta believe in something bigger and greater than all this mess we're in. I know religion is declining all over the world, and maybe that's good. Maybe a revival can come from the ashes and start fresh what religion messed up in the first place. People are shocked that I go to Europe so much to do concerts. They know that the churches there are closing and the people there are not open about what they believe. But when I go to Europe, I see something totally different—and I know other Christian artists do as well. Man, the people come out in the thousands to hear this music. To God's glory, I've sold out concerts in Amsterdam at the Heineken Arena. They're selling liquor while I'm pouring out God's love!

And I see the same thing in Asia. Not to boast on myself, but we're blessed by God to sing four nights in a row in Tokyo, and no one in the audience looks like me! They can't even speak English well, but they know the songs. They're singing, "Jesus," and lifting up their hands, even though they may not fully understand the message. But I'm like my boy Paul and my dude Apollos: I plant and water, but God gives the increase.

I see it every time I cross the oceans—the hunger and the love in Hungary, in Denmark, in France, in Stockholm, in São Paulo, on and on. I see it! Hungry people wanting something more than just rules, more than empty talk, more than empty lives; they want that Jesus, baby! The hope that comes from knowing that when I take my last breath and they put dirt over the casket and say farewell for the last time, I ain't even dead long enough to know it! 'Cause to be absent from this body . . .

I must be honest. Since I started writing this book, I've written with a thorn. I limp, having to carry a weight that is heavier than anything I've ever faced before in my life. As I write, the pen gets heavier because I am laboring with these burdens in my own life while I am also striving to give hope to someone else. I've always been honest about my family, about the fact that many people related to me have hurt me and still hurt me deeply. If not for the love and support of my beautiful wife, and the family we share together, I would be even crazier than I already am. It is hard when you pray for something, especially for some level of peace, and things don't change. Some things about love I will never understand, but I've come to see it as increasingly important that we understand love to be an action, not just a statement.

Since I don't want to ramble, I'll cut to the chase. If you wait for things to get better before you fly, before you live, before you enjoy the life you've been given, you probably will end up waiting a long time. I sit here at 1:20 in the morning fighting back tears because I look through a window that has so many cracks and am reminded daily to see every crack as another reason for needing a savior.

If you've endured—or are *still* enduring—circumstances so piercing that even blinking hurts, my sunshiny statements may lead you to shake your fist at the heavens to curse God and the day you were born. I understand that; I really do. But if you wait for world peace mixed with global cooling in a bowl where Republicans and Democrats sing "Kumbaya" together—well, you'll be gray and wearing Depends before that happens.

My brothers and sisters, you cannot wait for the rain to stop before you go outside to play. If the rain, the mother, the sickness, the son, the accident, the marriage is a cross given to you to keep you dependent, humble, and hungry, then welcome to a level of joy that most people never experience. Why does He allow these things when He claims to love us? I think I understand the reasons for some of them, but for others I believe only time will reveal the mystery of trials. Still, I know that without them we could not feel the passion in your songs, the depth in your writings, the integrity in your business, the level of excellence in everything you do. Your touch is softer because your hands hurt from holding on for dear life. Your speech is kind and endearing because each night you lose your voice crying to the heavens to heal your home. You're quick to lend to anyone in trouble because you see yourself as a beggar who has been given the bread of life.

Why He allows these things we don't always know. But if that is the secret to the internal strength I see in your eyes when you stand to speak, it somehow begins to make sense.

A couple's sleep was interrupted by screams that came from across the hall. It was four in the morning and their eight-year-old son's voice rang out as he pleaded for his father to come to his bedside. When the father ran to see the reason for his son's cries, he found the boy soaked from a fever that made it almost impossible even to touch him. Terrified by this discovery, the father grabbed his son and ran downstairs, prepared to break every driving law for the sake of his son's life. Racing through the doors of the emergency room, he made his presence known to everyone within his reach.

In response to the father's pleas, a physician called a team of professionals together to move the child directly into emergency surgery. The doctor informed the father that the cause was so dangerous that they couldn't waste any time or the boy wouldn't make it. After asking the father to hold the young boy down, the doctor began the risky procedure. Every time the doctor touched him, the child screamed with tears in his voice, pleading, "Daddy, make him stop!" The father tried to encourage the boy through the pain, but it didn't help. The boy would simply scream again, "Daddy, *PLEEAASE* make him stop!" But the father just wiped his own tears and found the courage inside himself to tell his son to hold on. When none of his cries won any relief, the boy's screams grew louder. Filled with pain, he cried out again, this time with a deep need to understand. "Daddy," he said, "if you love me, why won't you make him stop?"

Speechless and with nothing piercing the silence except the sound of hospital machinery, the father in the most broken part of his soul responded, "Son, I know this hurts, but it is the *only* way that you can get better."

I use this story as an illustration, an answer to the question that seems to obsess and frustrate us humans, *Why does He let bad things happen to good people?*

I know. I know the pain that causes the room to spin out of control in the wee hours of the morning. I know the loneliness of walking the streets all night long trying to hurt yourself physically, cursing God with each step.

And you know, too. The bitter taste of being cheated on, deceived and lied to for most of your life. The touch in your youth that was inappropriate and took your innocence forever.

You know. And you also know how, in the middle of the "wreck," you stuck your head out life's window and cried, "Daddy, if you love me, why won't you make it stop? How can you love me and hurt me at the same time?"

If you've never been there before in your cute little Christian life, keep living! There is a darkness in the night of pain that human eyes can't even adjust to see.

And in that darkness the smallest light can change the whole room.

It is painful, but it is necessary.

It is necessary for the caterpillar to go through the pushing and kicking that frees him from the cocoon in order to develop the muscles in his wings that he needs to fly.

It is necessary for a woman to go through the discomfort and pain of nine months, finally pushing in agony when the time for birth comes, when it's time for a new life to make her presence fully known.

It is painful, but it is necessary.

It is necessary for some of us to have trouble, to carry burdens in life, because those troubles and burdens push us down to our knees and pray. I believe the reason most of us don't get our prayers answered quickly is because God enjoys hearing our voices. It's not very often he gets to hear from us—unless, that is, we are in trouble. He already has the answer, but He enjoys the company.

For some of you, what I've said will never be enough. Many people turn away from God because of life's big "why" questions. Or because of the anger they feel toward God for allowing them to hurt so bad without stopping it.

Neither I nor anyone else will ever be able to reach into a person's heart and turn their response dial. That is between them and God.

So tonight, at three in the morning, I choose to write to you as I weep for people close to me—for my own flesh and blood, for the world, and for these kids. But as I hurt, I also have hope. As God gives me songs that speak to others when I struggle to get through my own difficult days, I choose to believe that His grace is sufficient. In the face of everything—being laughed at, written off, considered weird, abandoned, homeless, broke, no family, hurt by family, depressed, afraid of dying, afraid of living— His grace *is* sufficient. And if I must boast, I will boast in the things that show my weakness . . . *for I was given a thorn to keep me from being proud and conceited. And three times I asked the Lord to take it away. But he said "my grace is all you need." So I rejoice. For when I am weak, then I am strong* (Paul, AD 54, and Kirk, AD 2010).

For all my people in the struggle, I hope my failures and lessons can add to your blueprint. Or perhaps even be a blueprint for your journey. What will you build? What will you leave your children? What will your legacy be? Are you closer to knowing who you are? I have no more illustrations, and you're probably worn out with the ones I've put before you! All I have is a simple close. . . .

I wish Gertrude were here. I wish she could read these pages. I wish she could see that the seed she planted finally did take root and grow. I wish she could see the man God is building on her foundation. I wish I could tell her I'm sorry for being such a bad, lost little kid. I wish she could see these kids of mine. They are Franklins because she changed my name. By giving me hers. I owe her. I've been adopted twice! Imagine me!

Acknowledgments

I read my first book at age twenty-six. Now I'm writing thank-yous in a book that I wrote! That's incredible to me. What's even more incredible is all of the people who have been a part of that journey. Thank you for letting me read the pages of your lives.

Thank you, Tammy, for being my greatest and most humbling course.

Thank you to my "home work," my four beautiful children, Kerrion, Carrington, Kennedy, Caziah; to my team that covers me on and off the field, Carla, Jessie, Ron, Bonnie, Nina; to those special players, Paradigm Agency, Lydia Wells, Alyssa Reuben, Jason Yarn, and my main man, Michael van Dyck. These guys right here helped finish that final paper so I could graduate on time: Nick Chiles and Dr. Doug Blunt. I am forever thankful for your investment in this book. Everyone at Gotham: Lauren Marino, Beth Parker, and Lisa Johnson. Thank you so much for walking me through this new world; hope I make you proud. To all of the pastors, churches, and those who have followed my music, I thank you and I hope that the words you read will reflect every song you've heard. Gerald, Pastor West, Gertrude: thank you. Rest in Him.

051269992